The Impatient Baker

The Impatient Baker

✦

*Simple, Streamlined, and Speedy Recipes
for Classic American Baking*

Karlene Tillie, M.Ed
Author of *American Cookies*

iUniverse, Inc.
New York Lincoln Shanghai

The Impatient Baker
Simple, Streamlined, and Speedy Recipes for Classic American Baking

iUniverse books may be ordered through booksellers or by contacting:

iUniverse
2021 Pine Lake Road, Suite 100
Lincoln, NE 68512
www.iuniverse.com
1-800-Authors (1-800-288-4677)

The views expressed in this work are solely those of the author and do not necessarily reflect the views of the publisher, and the publisher hereby disclaims any responsibility for them.

ISBN: 978-0-595-45187-6 (pbk)
ISBN: 978-0-595-89494-9 (ebk)

Printed in the United States of America

To Andy, Alexander and Katharine

The sweetest ingredients in my life.

Contents

The Three Secrets to Successful Baking

1. Use the freshest ingredients you can get your hands on. Check the expiration dates on your flour, baking soda, baking powder and eggs. Smell your spices, butter and milk. They will taste as good as they smell.

2. Make sure your oven temperature is on target. An oven thermometer is a tiny investment to make for the enormous rewards of perfectly baked treats.

3. Follow recipes carefully. After every step, check off each ingredient to make sure it was added. Leaving out something as little as baking soda can ruin an entire batch of cookies.

The Way to Fast and Easy Baking

1. Put your flour, sugar, brown sugar and powdered sugar into wide-topped containers. And keep them in a handy location. Then you can scoop your measuring cups into them quickly and easily.

2. To soften butter quickly for a recipe, set it on a plate, cut it into 1-inch chunks, and microwave for about 10 seconds, or until the butter begins to soften, but doesn't melt. (You can do this with cream cheese, too.)

3. Use dishwasher-safe baking pans, measuring spoons and cups so you don't have to wash them by hand. Use parchment paper on cookie sheets.

Snappy Cakes

Creamy-Frosted Vanilla Butter Cake

Simple butter cake with luscious cream cheese frosting.

½ cup (1 stick) butter, softened
¾ cup sugar
2 eggs
½ cup milk
1 teaspoon vanilla extract
1 cup flour
1 teaspoon baking powder
¼ teaspoon salt (omit if using salted butter)
frosting-
6 ounces (three-quarters of a package) cream cheese, softened
2 tablespoons butter, softened
1 ½ cups confectioners' sugar
1 teaspoon vanilla extract

1. Preheat the oven to 350 degrees. Coat an 8-inch square or 9-inch round cake pan with non-stick cooking spray. In a large mixing bowl beat the butter and sugar for half a minute. Add the eggs, milk and vanilla and beat until smooth.

2. Sift the flour, baking powder and salt over the batter and beat on low speed until the batter is smooth. Pour into the pan and bake for 20-25 minutes or until the cake turns brown around the edges and a toothpick comes out dry when inserted into the center. Let the cake cool in the pan for 10 minutes and then turn out onto a rack to cool completely.

3. To make the frosting, beat the cream cheese and butter for 1 minute. Add the confectioners' sugar and vanilla and beat on low speed until the sugar is blended in. Then turn the mixer up to high and beat for 1 minute, or until the frosting is light and fluffy.

Vanilla Coffee-Frosted Spice Cake

Got a little extra coffee in the pot? Let it give this cake a jolt of flavor.

2 eggs
½ cup canola or vegetable oil
¾ cup sugar
2 teaspoons vanilla extract
½ cup strong coffee
1-1/3 cups flour
1 teaspoon ground cinnamon
½ teaspoon ground nutmeg
¼ teaspoon ground cloves
1 teaspoon baking powder
¼ teaspoon salt
frosting-
2 cups confectioners' sugar
2 tablespoons strong coffee
1 teaspoon vanilla extract
2 tablespoons melted butter

1. Preheat the oven to 350 degrees. Coat an 8-inch square or 9-inch round cake pan with non-stick cooking spray. In a large mixing bowl whisk the eggs. Add the oil, sugar, vanilla and coffee and whisk again until blended.

2. Sift the flour, spices, baking powder and salt over the bowl and gently whisk until the batter is smooth. Pour into the pan and bake for 25-30 minutes or until a toothpick comes out dry when inserted into the center. When the cake has cooled, top with the frosting.

3. To make the frosting, beat the confectioners' sugar, coffee, vanilla and butter until smooth and creamy. Add more sugar if too runny, more coffee if too stiff.

Comfy Coffee Cake

A light, cinnamon-kissed coffee cake.

topping-
½ cup sugar
½ cup flour
1 teaspoon ground cinnamon
6 tablespoons butter, melted
cake-
1 egg
¼ cup canola or vegetable oil
½ cup sugar
1/3 cup milk
1 teaspoon vanilla extract
1 cup flour
1 teaspoon baking powder
¼ teaspoon salt

1. Preheat the oven to 350 degrees. Coat a 9-inch round or 8-inch square baking pan with non-stick cooking spray. To make the topping, mix together the sugar, flour and cinnamon. Stir in the melted butter and set aside.

2. In a large mixing bowl whisk the egg. Add the oil, sugar, milk and vanilla and whisk until blended. Sift the flour and baking powder over the batter and gently whisk until the flour disappears (the batter will be lumpy).

3. Pour and spread the batter into the pan. Sprinkle with the topping and bake for 25-30 minutes or until the cake turns brown around the edges and a toothpick comes out dry when inserted into the center.

Cinnamon-Buttered Pecan Crumb Cake

Soft butter cake topped with firm brown-sugared pecans.

topping-
2/3 cup brown sugar
½ cup flour
1 teaspoon ground cinnamon
¼ teaspoon salt (omit if using salted butter)
6 tablespoons butter, melted
1 cup chopped pecans
cake-
1 large egg
¾ cup sugar
6 tablespoons butter, melted
½ cup milk
1 teaspoon vanilla extract
1 ¼ cups flour
1 ½ teaspoons baking powder
¼ teaspoon salt (omit if using salted butter)

1. Preheat the oven to 350 degrees. Coat a 9-inch round or 8-inch square baking pan with non-stick cooking spray. To make the topping, whisk together the brown sugar, flour, cinnamon and salt. Stir in the melted butter and pecans and set aside.

2. In a large mixing bowl whisk the egg. Add the sugar, melted butter, milk and vanilla and whisk until blended. Sift the flour, baking powder and salt over the bowl and gently whisk until the flour disappears (the batter will be lumpy).

3. Pour the batter into the pan and sprinkle the pecan mixture over the top. Bake for 25-30 minutes or until the edges of the cake turn brown and a toothpick comes out dry when inserted into the center.

Buttermilk-Brown Sugar Crumb Cake

Buttermilk makes this cake extra soft.

topping-
2/3 cup brown sugar
½ cup flour
1 teaspoon ground cinnamon
6 tablespoons butter, melted
cake-
1 egg
¼ cup canola oil
¾ cup sugar
1 cup buttermilk
1 teaspoon vanilla extract
1 ½ cups flour
1 teaspoon baking powder
½ teaspoon salt

1. Preheat the oven to 350 degrees. Coat a 9-inch round or 8-inch square baking pan with non-stick cooking spray. Whisk together the brown sugar, flour and cinnamon. Stir in the melted butter and set aside.

2. In a large mixing bowl, whisk the egg. Add the oil, sugar, buttermilk and vanilla and whisk until blended. Sift the flour, baking powder and salt over the bowl and gently whisk until the flour disappears (the batter will be lumpy).

3. Pour and spread the batter into the pan, sprinkle with the topping, and bake for 25-30 minutes or until a toothpick comes out dry when inserted into the center of the cake.

Chocolate Spice Cake with Red Wine Glaze

Chocolate cheers!

5—1 ounce squares unsweetened baking chocolate (like Baker's)
1 cup (2 sticks) butter, softened
¾ cup sugar
¾ cup brown sugar
4 eggs
1 cup milk
2 teaspoons vanilla extract
2 cups plus 2 tablespoons flour
2 teaspoons ground cinnamon
¼ teaspoon ground cloves
2 teaspoons baking powder
½ teaspoon salt (omit if using salted butter)
glaze-
2/3 cup semi-sweet chocolate chips
¼ cup good red wine

1. Preheat the oven to 350 degrees. Coat a bundt or tube pan with non-stick cooking spray. In a small saucepan, melt the chocolate over medium heat, stirring continuously until melted. Remove the pan from the heat and set aside.

2. In a large mixing bowl, beat the butter, sugar and brown sugar for half a minute. Beat in the eggs two at a time. Beat in the melted chocolate. Add the milk and vanilla and beat until well blended. Sift the flour, cinnamon, cloves, baking powder and salt over the bowl and beat on low speed until the batter is smooth.

3. Pour and spread the batter into the pan and bake for 40-50 minutes or until a toothpick comes out dry when inserted into the center of the cake. Cool in the pan for 15 minutes, then turn out onto a rack to cool completely. To make the glaze, melt the chocolate chips in a saucepan over medium heat. Remove the pan from the heat and slowly whisk in the red wine, whisking until smooth (It might take a minute of whisking to smooth out.) Pour and spread over the cooled cake.

<u>Chocolate Coffee Cake</u>

Cocoa powder and chocolate chips take coffee cake to a luxurious level.

topping-
½ cup sugar
½ cup flour
6 tablespoons butter, melted
1 teaspoon vanilla extract
½ cup semi-sweet chocolate chips
cake-
2 eggs
½ cup canola or vegetable oil
½ cup sugar
¼ cup brown sugar
¾ cup milk
1 teaspoon vanilla extract
1 ¼ cups flour
¼ cup unsweetened cocoa powder
1 ½ teaspoons baking powder
¼ teaspoon salt

1. Preheat the oven to 350 degrees. Coat an 8-inch square or 9-inch round baking pan with non-stick cooking spray. To make the topping, whisk the sugar and flour together. Stir in the melted butter and vanilla. Toss in the chocolate chips and set aside.

2. In a large mixing bowl, whisk the eggs. Add the oil, sugar, brown sugar, milk and vanilla and whisk until blended.

3. Sift the flour, cocoa powder, baking powder and salt over the bowl and gently whisk until the flour mixture disappears (the batter will be lumpy). Pour the batter into the pan, sprinkle with the topping mixture, and bake for 30-35 minutes or until a toothpick comes out dry when inserted into the center of the cake.

Fudgie-Wudgie Pudding Cake

Chocolate heaven.

1 cup flour
¼ cup unsweetened cocoa powder
¾ cup sugar
1 teaspoon baking powder
¼ teaspoon salt
½ cup milk
3 teaspoons butter, melted
1 teaspoon vanilla extract
topping-
½ cup brown sugar
¼ cup unsweetened cocoa powder
½ cup semi-sweet chocolate chips
1 ¼ cups hot water

1. Preheat the oven to 350 degrees. Coat an 8-inch square baking pan with non-stick cooking spray. In a large mixing bowl, whisk the first 5 dry ingredients. Add the milk, melted butter and vanilla and gently whisk until the flour disappears (the batter will be lumpy).

2. Pour the batter into the pan. To make the topping, stir together the brown sugar, cocoa powder and chocolate chips until well combined. Sprinkle over the batter. Then pour the hot water over the entire pan. Do not stir.

3. Bake for 25-30 minutes or until most of the top is firm and no longer liquid. (Portions of the top will be wet and fudgy.) Cool for 20 minutes in the pan. Serve warm and top with a bit of the chocolate sauce from the pan. Serve with a scoop of vanilla ice cream or whipped cream.

Spooky-Dark Chocolate Cake

This chocolate cake will move your spirit.

4 eggs
1 cup canola or vegetable oil
1 cup brown sugar
¾ cup sugar
1 cup coffee
2 teaspoons vanilla extract
2 ¼ cups flour
¾ cup unsweetened cocoa powder
1 ½ teaspoons baking powder
1 teaspoon salt
chocolate glaze—
2/3 cup semi-sweet chocolate chips
2 tablespoons milk
2 tablespoons butter

1. Preheat the oven to 350 degrees. Coat a 10-inch bundt or tube pan with non-stick cooking spray. In a large mixing bowl whisk the eggs. Whisk in the oil, brown sugar, sugar, coffee and vanilla. Sift <u>1 cup</u> of the flour, the cocoa powder, baking powder and salt over the bowl and whisk until the batter is smooth. Sift in the remaining flour and <u>gently</u> whisk until the flour disappears.

2. Pour and spread the batter into the pan and bake for 35-40 minutes or until a toothpick comes out dry when inserted into the center of the cake. After 10 minutes, turn the cake out onto a cooling rack.

3. To make the glaze, put the chocolate chips, milk and butter into a small sauce pan over medium heat. Stir until the chocolate has melted and the mixture is smooth. When the glaze is no longer hot, drizzle it over the cooled cake.

Chocolate Buttermilk Cake with Cocoa Glaze

Tender cake filled with rich cocoa flavor.

2 eggs
½ cup (1 stick) butter, melted
½ cup brown sugar
½ cup sugar
1 teaspoon vanilla extract
2/3 cup buttermilk
1 cup flour
¼ cup unsweetened cocoa powder
1/2 teaspoon baking powder
1/4 teaspoon salt (omit if using salted butter)
glaze-
2 cups confectioners' sugar
5 tablespoons unsweetened cocoa powder
¼ cup (half a stick) melted butter
5 tablespoons warm milk
1 teaspoon vanilla extract

1. Preheat the oven to 350 degrees. Coat a 9-inch round or 8-inch square baking pan with non-stick cooking spray. In a large mixing bowl, whisk the eggs. Add the melted butter, brown sugar, sugar and buttermilk and whisk until blended. Sift the flour, cocoa powder, baking powder and salt over the bowl and gently whisk until the batter is smooth.

2. Pour the batter into the pan and bake for 20-25 minutes or until a toothpick comes out dry when inserted into the center of the cake. After 10 minutes turn the cake out of the pan to cool completely.

3. To make the glaze, whisk together the confectioners' sugar and cocoa powder. Add the melted butter, warm milk and vanilla and whisk until smooth and creamy. (Add more confectioners' sugar if glaze is too runny, more milk if to stiff.) Pour and spread over the cooled cake.

I Love You Cake

A dark, passionate cake smothered in pure white frosting.

2 eggs
3/4 cup sugar
1/2 cup canola or vegetable oil
1/2 cup milk
1 teaspoon vanilla extract
1 ¼ cups flour
2 tablespoons unsweetened cocoa powder
1 teaspoon baking powder
¼ teaspoon salt
frosting-
1 ½ cups confectioners' sugar
2 tablespoons butter, melted
2 tablespoons warm milk
1 teaspoon vanilla extract

1. Preheat the oven to 350 degrees. Coat a heart-shaped cake pan, a 9-inch round or an 8-inch square baking pan with non-stick cooking spray. In a large mixing bowl, whisk the eggs. Add the sugar, oil, milk and vanilla and whisk until blended.

2. Sift the flour, cocoa powder, baking powder and salt over the bowl and gently whisk until smooth. Pour the batter into the pan and bake for 20-25 minutes or until a toothpick comes out dry when inserted into the center of the cake. Remove the cake from the pan after 10 minutes to cool completely.

3. To make the frosting, combine the confectioners' sugar, melted butter, warm milk and vanilla and whisk or beat until smooth and creamy (add more sugar if too runny, more milk if to stiff). Frost the cake and decorate with colored sprinkles, candy or write a loving message with decorator icing.

Double Chocolate Zucchini Cake

Zucchini is the best kept secret for a moist, low-fat cake.

1 egg
1/3 cup sugar
1/3 cup brown sugar
1/3 cup canola or vegetable oil
1/3 cup milk
1 teaspoon vanilla
1 cup flour
¼ cup unsweetened cocoa powder
½ teaspoon ground cinnamon
1 teaspoon baking powder
¼ teaspoon salt
1 cup shredded zucchini
2/3 cup semi-sweet chocolate chips
topping-
2 tablespoons sugar
2 teaspoons cocoa powder
½ teaspoon ground cinnamon

1. Preheat the oven to 350 degrees. Coat an 8-inch square or 9-inch round baking pan with non-stick cooking spray. In a large bowl, whisk the egg. Add the sugar, brown sugar, oil, milk and vanilla and whisk until smooth.

2. Sift the flour, cocoa powder, cinnamon, baking powder and salt over the bowl and gently whisk until the flour disappears (the batter will be lumpy). Gently stir in the zucchini and chocolate chips.

3. Pour and spread the batter into the pan. Stir the topping ingredients together and sprinkle over the top. Bake for 25-30 minutes or until a toothpick comes out dry when inserted into the center.

<u>Brownie Cake a la Mode</u>

A big chocolate brownie you eat with a spoon.

3—1 ounce squares unsweetened baking chocolate (like Baker's)
½ cup (1 stick) butter
¾ cup brown sugar
½ cup sugar
2 teaspoons vanilla extract
3 eggs
2/3 cup flour
1 teaspoon baking powder
¼ teaspoon salt (omit if using salted butter)
vanilla ice cream

1. Preheat the oven to 350 degrees. Coat an 8-inch square baking pan with non-stick cooking spray. In a small saucepan, melt the chocolate and butter over medium heat, stirring until melted. Pour into a large mixing bowl.

2. With a wire whisk, blend in the brown sugar, sugar and vanilla until smooth. Whisk in the eggs until the batter is smooth and glossy. Sift the flour, baking powder and salt over the bowl and whisk gently until the flour disappears.

3. Pour into the pan and bake for 25 minutes or until a toothpick comes out dry when inserted about <u>2-inches</u> from the edge of the baking pan. Cut into 9 squares and serve warm with a generous scoop of vanilla ice cream.

<u>Sugared Apple Cake</u>

Cinnamon-apple delicious.

sugared apples-
2 tablespoons sugar
2 teaspoons ground cinnamon
2-3 large apples, peeled, cored and cut into bite-sized bits (about 2 ½ cups)
cake-
1 egg
½ cup sugar
2/3 cup canola or vegetable oil
1/3 cup milk
1 teaspoon vanilla extract
1 ¼ cups flour
1 teaspoon baking powder
½ teaspoon salt
topping-
1 tablespoon sugar

1. Preheat the oven to 350 degrees. Coat an 8-inch square or 9-inch round baking pan with non-stick cooking spray. In a large bowl mix together the sugar and cinnamon. Add the apple pieces and toss until well coated. Set aside.

2. In a large mixing bowl, whisk the egg. Add the sugar, oil, milk and vanilla and whisk until blended. Sift the flour, baking powder and salt over the bowl and gently whisk until the flour disappears (the batter will be lumpy).

3. Pour and spread the batter into the pan, top with the sugared apples, and bake for 25-30 minutes or until the edges of the cake turn golden brown and a toothpick comes out dry when inserted into the center. Sprinkle 1 tablespoon of sugar over the baked cake.

Bumpy Blueberry Sour Cream Cake

Blueberries add delicious texture and color to this moist cake.

topping-
1/3 cup flour
1/3 cup sugar
½ teaspoon ground cinnamon
5 tablespoons butter, melted
cake-
1 egg
2/3 cup sugar
2/3 cup sour cream
1/3 cup canola or vegetable oil
1 teaspoon vanilla extract
1-1/3 cups flour
1 ½ teaspoons baking powder
1/4 teaspoon salt
1 cup blueberries
glaze-
1 cup confectioners' sugar
2 tablespoons warm milk

1. Preheat the oven to 350 degrees. Coat an 8-inch square or 9-inch round cake pan with non-stick cooking spray. To make the topping, blend the flour, sugar and cinnamon with a whisk. Add the melted butter and stir until well combined and crumbly. Set aside.

2. In a large mixing bowl, whisk the egg. Add the sugar, sour cream, oil and vanilla and whisk until blended. Sift the flour, baking powder and salt over the bowl and gently whisk until the flour disappears (the batter will be lumpy).

3. Pour and spread the batter into the pan, top with the blueberries, and then with the topping mixture. Bake for 25-30 minutes or until the cake begins to turn brown around the edges and a toothpick comes out dry when inserted into the center. To make the glaze, whisk the confectioners' sugar with the warm milk. (Add more milk if too stiff, more sugar if too runny.) Drizzle over the cooled cake.

<u>Cinnamon-Glazed Sugar Plum Cake</u>

Sugar plums are not plums but a blend of dried fruit, nuts and wintry spices.

1 cup sugar
¾ cup canola or vegetable oil
3 eggs
1 teaspoon vanilla extract
1 cup applesauce
2 cups flour
1 teaspoon ground cinnamon
½ teaspoon ground nutmeg
¼ teaspoon ground cloves
1 tablespoon baking powder
1 teaspoon salt
½ cup raisins
½ cup currents
1 cup chopped pecans
glaze-
1 ½ cups confectioners' sugar
½ teaspoon ground cinnamon
¼ cup warm milk
½ teaspoon vanilla extract

1. Preheat the oven to 350 degrees. Coat a 10-inch round bundt or tube cake pan with non-stick cooking spray. In a large mixing bowl, beat the sugar, oil and eggs for half a minute. Beat in the vanilla and applesauce.

2. Sift the flour, spices, baking powder and salt over the bowl and beat on low speed until the flour disappears. Gently fold in the raisins, currents and pecans. Pour and spread the batter into the pan and bake for 40-50 minutes or until a toothpick comes out dry when inserted into the center of the cake. Turn the cake out of the pan after 10 minutes to cool completely.

3. To make the glaze, whisk together the confectioners' sugar and cinnamon. Add the warm milk and vanilla and whisk until smooth and creamy. (Add more milk if too stiff, more sugar if too runny.) Drizzle over the cooled cake.

Cinnamon Plum Crumb Cake

Soft cake with a sugary plum topping.

topping-
½ cup flour
½ cup sugar
1 teaspoon ground cinnamon
6 tablespoons butter, melted
cake-
2 eggs
½ cup canola or vegetable oil
2/3 cup sugar
½ cup milk
1 teaspoon vanilla extract
1-1/3 cups flour
1 teaspoon baking powder
½ teaspoon salt
6 medium-sized plums, cut into half-inch slices

1. Preheat the oven to 350 degrees. Coat an 8-inch square or 9-inch round baking pan with non-stick cooking spray. To make the crumb topping, mix the flour, sugar and cinnamon until blended. Pour in the melted butter and blend with a fork until the mixture is well combined and crumbly. Set aside.

2. In a large mixing bowl, whisk the eggs. Add the oil, sugar, milk and vanilla and whisk until blended. Sift the flour, baking powder and salt over the bowl and gently whisk until blended (the batter will be lumpy).

3. Pour the batter into the pan, place the sliced plums on top, and then sprinkle the crumb topping over the plums. Bake for 30-35 minutes or until a toothpick comes out dry when inserted into the center of the cake.

Maple Butter-Glazed Apple Walnut Cake

Maple syrup glorifies the taste of apples and walnuts.

3 eggs
1 ½ cups sugar
1 cup canola or vegetable oil
1 teaspoon vanilla extract
1 ½ cups chunky applesauce
2 ½ cups flour
2 teaspoons cinnamon
½ teaspoon nutmeg
2 teaspoons baking powder
1 teaspoon salt
1 cup chopped walnuts
glaze-
¼ cup maple syrup
2 tablespoons melted butter
1 ½ cups confectioners' sugar

1. Preheat the oven to 350 degrees. Coat a bundt or tube baking pan with non-stick cooking spray. In a large bowl, whisk the eggs. Add the sugar, oil, and vanilla and whisk until blended. Whisk in the applesauce.

2. Sift the flour, cinnamon, nutmeg, baking powder and salt over the bowl and gently whisk until the flour disappears (the batter will be lumpy). Gently stir in the walnuts. Pour and spread the batter into the pan and bake for 45-50 minutes or until a toothpick comes out dry when inserted into the center.

3. To make the glaze, whisk together the syrup and butter. Add the confectioners' sugar and whisk until smooth. (Add more syrup if too stiff, more sugar if too runny.) Drizzle over the cooled cake.

Mandarin Orange Cake with Brown Sugar Glaze

A slice of this cake is like a serving of warm sunshine.

1 large egg
¾ cup sugar
1/3 cup canola or vegetable oil
1 teaspoon vanilla extract
¼ cup milk
1 ¼ cups flour
1 teaspoon baking powder
½ teaspoon salt
1—11 ounce can mandarin orange slices, drained
glaze—
¾ cup brown sugar
4 tablespoons (half a stick) butter
½ teaspoon vanilla extract

1. Preheat the oven to 350 degrees. Coat a 9-inch round or 8-inch square baking pan with non-stick cooking spray. In a large mixing bowl, whisk the egg. Add the sugar, oil, vanilla and milk and whisk until blended.

2. Sift the flour, baking powder and salt over the bowl and gently whisk until the flour disappears (the batter will be lumpy). Pour and spread the batter into the pan, set the orange slices on top, and bake for 30-35 minutes or until the cake is golden brown and a toothpick comes out dry when inserted into the center. After 10 minutes, turn the cake out to cool completely.

3. To make the glaze, place the brown sugar and butter into a small saucepan and stir over medium-high heat. While stirring, bring the mixture to a full boil. Once the sugar has dissolved, remove the pan from the heat and whisk in the vanilla. When the glaze is no longer hot, pour over the top of the cake.

Pineapple Upside-down Skillet Cake

Brown-sugared pineapples top a soft, simple cake.

½ cup (1 stick) butter
½ cup brown sugar
1 large can sliced pineapple rings
10 maraschino cherries
1 cup pecan halves
2 eggs
2/3 cup sugar
1/3 cup pineapple juice (from the canned pineapple)
1 teaspoon vanilla extract
1 cup flour
½ teaspoon baking powder
¼ teaspoon salt (omit if using salted butter)

1. Preheat the oven to 350 degrees. Melt the butter in a cast iron or heavy 10-inch skillet. Remove the pan from the heat and sprinkle the brown sugar over the butter. Arrange the pineapple slices in a circle around the edges of the pan and place one in the center. Set a cherry into the middle of each pineapple ring. Fill in the spaces between the pineapples with pecan halves. Set aside.

2. In a large mixing bowl, whisk the eggs. Add the sugar, pineapple juice and vanilla and whisk until blended. Sift the flour, baking powder and salt over the bowl and gently whisk until the flour disappears (the batter will be lumpy).

3. Pour and spread the batter over the pineapples. Bake for 25-30 minutes or until the cake turns golden brown. Let the pan cool for 5 minutes, then flip it upside down onto a serving plate and let it sit and settle for about 5 minutes. Remove the pan. Serve warm with vanilla ice cream or whipped cream.

<u>Cinnamon Apple Coffee Cake</u>

The best part of this cake is the cinnamon-sugar topping.

topping-
1/3 cup flour
1/3 cup brown sugar
1/3 cup sugar
1 teaspoon ground cinnamon
¼ teaspoon salt (omit if using salted butter)
1 cup peeled, cored and chopped apples
6 tablespoons butter, melted
cake-
1 egg
½ cup sugar
1/3 cup canola or vegetable oil
1 teaspoon vanilla extract
½ cup milk
1 ¼ cups flour
1 ½ teaspoons baking powder
¼ teaspoon salt

1. Preheat the oven to 350 degrees. Coat a 9-inch round or 8-inch square pan with non-stick cooking spray. To make the topping, whisk the flour, brown sugar, sugar, cinnamon and salt until blended. Stir in the apples. Then pour the butter over the mixture and toss until well combined. Set aside.

2. In a large mixing bowl, whisk the egg. Add the sugar, oil, vanilla and milk and whisk until blended. Sift the flour, baking powder and salt over the bowl and gently whisk until the flour disappears (the batter will be lumpy).

3. Pour and spread the batter into the pan, sprinkle the apple mixture evenly over the top, and bake for 25-30 minutes or until the cake turns golden brown around the edges and a toothpick comes out dry when inserted into the center.

Strawberry Cinnamon Coffee Cake

Bright red strawberries are ravishing in this delightful cake.

topping-
1/3 cup flour
1/3 cup sugar
1 teaspoon ground cinnamon
5 tablespoons butter, melted
cake-
2 eggs
2/3 cup sugar
2/3 cup canola or vegetable oil
2/3 cup milk
1 teaspoon vanilla extract
1 ¼ cups flour
1 teaspoon baking powder
½ teaspoon salt
¾ cup strawberries, cut into bite sized pieces

1. Preheat the oven to 350 degrees. Coat a 9-inch round or 8-inch square baking pan with non-stick cooking spray. To make the topping, blend the flour, sugar and cinnamon with a whisk. Stir in the melted butter and set aside.

2. In a large mixing bowl, whisk the eggs. Add the sugar, oil, milk and vanilla and whisk until blended. Sift the flour, baking powder and salt over the bowl and gently whisk until the flour disappears (the batter will be lumpy).

3. Pour and spread the batter into the pan. Sprinkle the strawberries over the top, then sprinkle the topping mixture over the strawberries. Bake for 25-30 minutes or until the edges turn golden brown and a toothpick comes out dry when inserted into the center.

Blueberry Almond Streusel Crumb Cake

Crunchy almonds and soft blueberries are a sumptuous match.

topping-
½ cup sugar
1/3 cup flour
½ teaspoon ground cinnamon
5 tablespoons butter, melted
1/3 cup chopped or sliced almonds
cake-
2 eggs
½ cup canola or vegetable oil
¾ cup sugar
¾ cup milk
1 teaspoon vanilla extract
1 ½ cups flour
2 teaspoons baking powder
½ teaspoon salt
1 cup blueberries

1. Preheat the oven to 350 degrees. Coat an 8-inch square or 9-inch round baking pan with non-stick cooking spray. To make the topping, blend the sugar, flour and cinnamon with a whisk. Stir in the melted butter and almonds and set aside.

2. In a large mixing bowl, whisk the eggs. Add the oil, sugar, milk and vanilla and whisk until blended. Sift the flour, baking powder and salt over the bowl and gently whisk until the flour disappears (the batter will be lumpy).

3. Pour and spread the batter into the pan, sprinkle with the blueberries, then with the topping mixture. Bake for 30-35 minutes or until cake turns brown around the edges and a toothpick comes out dry when inserted into the center.

Rum Cake with Apples

The lovable flavors of apple, brown sugar and cinnamon tweaked with rum.

topping-
1/3 cup brown sugar
1/3 cup flour
1 teaspoon ground cinnamon
1 cup apple pieces (cut into bite-sized bits)
5 tablespoons butter, melted
cake-
2 eggs
1 cup sugar
½ cup canola or vegetable oil
½ cup milk
¼ cup rum
2 teaspoons vanilla extract
1 ¾ cups flour
2 teaspoons baking powder
½ teaspoon salt
rum glaze—(optional)
1 ½ cups confectioners' sugar
2 tablespoons rum
3 tablespoons butter, melted

1. Preheat the oven to 350 degrees. Coat a 10-inch round springform pan with non-stick cooking spray. To make the topping, whisk the brown sugar, flour and cinnamon until blended. Stir in the apple pieces. Then add the melted butter and toss until well blended. Set aside.

2. In a large mixing bowl, whisk the eggs. Add the sugar, oil, milk, rum and vanilla and whisk until blended. Sift the flour, baking powder and salt over the bowl and gently whisk until the batter is smooth.

3. Pour and spread the batter into the pan, sprinkle with the topping mixture, and bake for 30-35 minutes or until the cake turns brown around the edges and a toothpick comes out dry when inserted into the center. To make the rum glaze, whisk the confectioners' sugar, rum and melted butter until smooth. (Add more sugar if too runny, more rum if too stiff.) Pour and spread over the cake.

<u>Orange Sunshine Cake</u>

It's not a trip to Florida, but this cake will take your taste buds there.

4 eggs
¾ cup canola or vegetable oil
1-1/3 cups sugar
½ cup orange juice
2 teaspoons vanilla extract
1 teaspoon orange or lemon extract
2 cups flour
2 teaspoons baking powder
½ teaspoon salt
glaze-
3 tablespoons butter, melted
3 tablespoons warm orange juice
1 teaspoon vanilla extract
2 cups confectioners' sugar
2 drops yellow food coloring (optional)

1. Preheat the oven to 350 degrees. Coat a bundt or tube cake pan with non-stick cooking spray. In a large mixing bowl, whisk the eggs. Add the oil, sugar, orange juice and extracts and whisk until blended.

2. Sift the flour, baking powder and salt over the bowl and gently whisk until the flour disappears (the batter will be lumpy). Pour into pan and bake for 30-35 minutes or until a toothpick comes out dry when inserted into the center. Cool for 10 minutes then turn the cake out to cool completely.

3. To make the glaze, whisk together all of the glaze ingredients until smooth and creamy. (Add more juice if too stiff, more sugar if too runny.) Drizzle over the cooled cake.

Irish Apple Cake

A charming cake filled with apples and cinnamon.

1 large egg
1/3 cup canola or vegetable oil
2/3 cup sugar
½ cup milk
1 teaspoon vanilla extract
1 ¼ cups flour
1 teaspoon ground cinnamon
1 ½ teaspoons baking powder
¼ teaspoon salt
4 apples, peeled, cored and cut into bite-sized pieces (about 2 cups)
topping-
2 tablespoons sugar
1 teaspoon ground cinnamon

1. Preheat the oven to 350 degrees. Coat a 9-inch round or 8-inch square baking pan with non-stick cooking spray. In a large mixing bowl, whisk the egg. Add the oil, sugar, milk and vanilla and whisk until blended.

2. Sift the flour, cinnamon, baking powder and salt over the bowl and gently whisk until the flour disappears (the batter will be lumpy). Gently fold in the apples.

3. Pour and spread the batter into the pan. Blend the topping ingredients together and sprinkle <u>1 tablespoon of the mixture</u> over the cake. Bake for 30-35 minutes or until the cake turns light brown and a toothpick comes out dry when inserted into the center. Sprinkle the rest of the cinnamon-sugar over the cake. Serve with whipped cream or vanilla ice cream.

Brown Sugar Rhubarb Cake

Brown sugar brings out the best in fresh, tart rhubarb.

topping-
½ cup brown sugar
¼ cup flour
½ teaspoon ground cinnamon
5 tablespoons butter, melted
cake-
1 egg
1/3 cup canola or vegetable oil
¾ cup sugar
1/3 cup milk
1 teaspoon vanilla extract
1 cup flour
1 teaspoon baking powder
¼ teaspoon salt
1 cup finely chopped rhubarb

1. Preheat the oven to 350 degrees. Coat an 8-inch square or 9-inch round baking pan with non-stick cooking spray. Whisk together the brown sugar, flour and cinnamon. Add the melted butter and stir until well combined and crumbly. Set aside.

2. In a large mixing bowl, whisk the egg. Add the oil, sugar, milk and vanilla and whisk until blended. Sift the flour, baking powder and salt over the bowl and gently whisk until the flour disappears (the batter will be lumpy). Gently fold in the rhubarb.

3. Pour and spread the batter into the pan, sprinkle with the topping mixture, and bake for 25-30 minutes or until the cake turns brown around the edges and a toothpick comes out dry when inserted into the center.

Apple Cake a la Mode

Baked apples yearn for vanilla ice cream.

topping-
1 tablespoon sugar
2 tablespoons brown sugar
½ teaspoon ground cinnamon
3 large apples, peeled, cored and cut into bite-sized bits (about 2 ½ cups)
cake-
1 egg
½ cup sugar
1/3 cup canola or vegetable oil
1/3 cup milk
1 teaspoon vanilla extract
1 cup flour
1 teaspoon baking powder
¼ teaspoon salt
¼ cup (half a stick) butter, melted
vanilla ice cream

1. Preheat the oven to 350 degrees. Coat a 9-inch round or 8-inch square baking pan with non-stick cooking spray. In a large bowl, whisk together the sugar, brown sugar and cinnamon. Add the apples and toss until evenly coated. Set aside.

2. In a large mixing bowl, whisk the egg. Add the sugar, oil, milk and vanilla and whisk until blended. Sift the flour, baking powder and salt over the bowl and gently whisk until the flour disappears (the batter will be lumpy).

3. Pour and spread the batter into the pan and top with the sugared apples. Pour the melted butter evenly over the top and bake for 25-30 minutes or until the cake turns golden brown around the edges. Serve warm with vanilla ice cream.

Cinnamon-Sugared Gingerbread Cake

Gingerbread with an irresistible butter topping.

2 eggs
1 cup dark brown sugar
¾ cup canola or vegetable oil
½ cup milk
1 teaspoon vanilla extract
1 ½ cups flour
1 teaspoon ground ginger
1 teaspoon ground cinnamon
¼ teaspoon ground cloves
1 teaspoon baking powder
½ teaspoon salt
1/3 cup soft raisins (optional)
topping—
½ teaspoon ground cinnamon
2 tablespoons sugar
4 tablespoons (half a stick) butter, melted

1. Preheat the oven to 350 degrees. Coat an 8-inch square or 9-inch round baking pan with non-stick cooking spray. In a large mixing bowl, whisk the eggs. Add the brown sugar, oil, milk and vanilla and whisk again until blended.

2. Sift the flour, spices, baking powder and salt over the bowl and gently whisk until the flour disappears (the batter will be lumpy). Fold in the raisins, if using. Pour the batter into the pan and bake for 25-30 minutes or until the cake begins to brown around the edges and a toothpick comes out dry when inserted into the center.

3. To make the topping, stir the cinnamon into the sugar and set aside. Spread half of the melted butter over the cake. (A pastry brush works well here.) When the butter sets (after 1-2 minutes) spread the rest of the butter over the top and immediately sprinkle the cinnamon-sugar over the buttered top.

Chocolate-Black Tea Cake

This requires a little melting and steeping but the taste is worth the extra few minutes.

½ cup (1 stick) butter
2—1 ounce squares unsweetened baking chocolate (like Baker's)
2 bags of black tea
2 eggs
½ cup sugar
½ cup brown sugar
1 ¼ cups flour
1 teaspoon baking powder
½ teaspoon salt (omit if using salted butter)
glaze-
¾ cup semi-sweet chocolate chips
3 tablespoons butter
1 tablespoon light corn syrup

1. Preheat the oven to 350 degrees. Coat a 9-inch round or 8-inch square baking pan with non-stick cooking spray. Over medium heat, melt the butter and chocolate. Set aside. Place the 2 tea bags into one-half cup of hot water and let steep for 5 minutes.

2. In a large mixing bowl, whisk the eggs. Add the sugar, brown sugar, chocolate and tea and whisk until blended. Sift the flour, baking powder and salt over the bowl and gently whisk until the flour disappears. Pour into the pan and bake for 20-25 minutes or until a toothpick comes out dry when inserted into the center of the cake. Turn the cake out after 10 minutes to cool completely.

3. To make the glaze, melt the chocolate chips, butter and corn syrup over medium heat, stirring until the mixture is melted and smooth. Pour and spread the glaze over the top of the cooled cake, letting it drizzle down the sides.

Pumpkin Carrot Cake

A delectable fall treat.

2 eggs
¾ cup sugar
½ cup canola oil
1 cup canned pumpkin
1 teaspoon vanilla extract
1 ¼ cups flour
1 teaspoon ground cinnamon
¼ teaspoon ground cloves
1 teaspoon baking powder
½ teaspoon salt
1 cup shredded carrots
½ cup chopped walnuts or semi-sweet chocolate chips (optional)

1. Preheat the oven to 350 degrees. Coat an 8-inch square or 9-inch round baking pan with non-stick cooking spray. In a large mixing bowl, whisk the eggs. Add the sugar, oil, pumpkin and vanilla and whisk until the mixture is smooth.

2. Sift the flour, cinnamon, cloves, baking powder and salt over the bowl and gently whisk until the flour disappears (the batter will be lumpy). Fold in the shredded carrots, and nuts or chocolate (if using).

3. Pour and spread the batter into the pan. Bake for 30-35 minutes or until a toothpick comes out dry when inserted into the center of the cake.

Honey Cake with Honey-Butter Glaze

Cinnamon and vanilla arouse the natural flavor of honey.

2 eggs
½ cup sugar
1/3 cup canola or vegetable oil
¼ cup honey
2 teaspoons vanilla extract
½ cup milk
1 ¼ cups flour
1 teaspoon ground cinnamon
1 teaspoon baking powder
½ teaspoon salt
glaze-
¼ cup honey
3 tablespoons butter, melted

1. Preheat the oven to 350 degrees. Coat an 8-inch square or 9-inch round cake pan with non-stick cooking spray. In a large mixing bowl, whisk the eggs. Add the sugar, oil, honey and vanilla and whisk until blended. Whisk in the milk.

2. Sift the flour, cinnamon, baking powder and salt over the bowl and gently whisk until the flour disappears (the batter will be lumpy).

3. Pour and spread the batter into the pan. Bake for 30-35 minutes or until the cake turns brown around the edges and a toothpick comes out dry when inserted into the center. Whisk together the honey and melted butter and drizzle over the cooled cake.

Cinnamon-Dusted Chocolate Chip Zucchini Cake

Eating your vegetables never tasted so good.

2 eggs
¾ cup sugar
½ cup canola or vegetable oil
1/3 cup milk
1 teaspoon vanilla extract
1 ¼ cups shredded zucchini
1 ½ cups flour
1 teaspoon ground cinnamon
1 teaspoon baking powder
½ teaspoon salt
¾ cup semi-sweet chocolate chips
topping-
1 tablespoon sugar
½ teaspoon ground cinnamon

1. Preheat the oven to 350 degrees. Coat an 8-inch square or 9-inch round baking pan with non-stick cooking spray. In a large mixing bowl, whisk the eggs. Add the sugar, oil, milk and vanilla and whisk until blended. Stir in the zucchini.

2. Sift the flour, cinnamon, baking powder and salt over the bowl and gently whisk until the flour disappears (the batter will be lumpy). Gently fold in the chocolate chips.

3. Pour and spread the batter into the pan. Bake for 25-30 minutes or until a toothpick comes out dry when inserted into the center. Blend the sugar and cinnamon together and sprinkle over the top.

Beer n' Spice Cake

Beer adds spunk to this spirited spice cake.

2 eggs
1 cup sugar
1/3 cup brown sugar
2/3 cup canola oil
1-1/3 cups beer (about 1 bottle)
2 cups flour
1 teaspoon ground cinnamon
½ teaspoon allspice
¼ teaspoon ground cloves
1 ½ teaspoons baking powder
½ teaspoon salt
2/3 cup chopped walnuts (optional)
2/3 cup raisins (optional)
cinnamon-drizzle icing-
2 cups confectioners' sugar
½ teaspoon ground cinnamon
2 tablespoons warm milk
2 tablespoons melted butter
¼ teaspoon vanilla extract

1. Preheat the oven to 350 degrees. Coat a 10-inch bundt or tube pan with non-stick cooking spray. In a large mixing bowl, whisk the eggs. Add the sugar, brown sugar and oil and whisk until blended. Slowly pour in the beer (so it doesn't foam up too much) and whisk again until blended.

2. Sift the flour, spices, baking powder and salt over the bowl and gently whisk until the flour disappears (the batter will be lumpy). Fold in the nuts and raisins, if using. Pour and spread the batter into the pan. Bake for 40-45 minutes or until a toothpick comes out dry when inserted into the center of the cake. Cool for 10 minutes and then turn out of the pan to cool completely.

3. To make the icing, whisk the confectioners' sugar, cinnamon, milk, melted butter and vanilla until smooth and creamy. (Add more sugar if too runny, more milk if too stiff.) Drizzle over the cooled cake.

Lighter-Side Carrot Cake

This recipe makes an easy-to-frost 9x13 inch cake.

3 eggs
1 cup sugar
¼ cup brown sugar
½ cup canola or vegetable oil
1 cup applesauce
2 cups flour
2 teaspoons ground cinnamon
¼ teaspoon ground cloves
2 teaspoons baking powder
1 teaspoon salt
3 cups shredded carrots
½ cup chopped walnuts or raisins
frosting-
1–8 ounce package Neufchatel cheese (1/3 less fat cream cheese), softened
½ cup (1 stick) butter, softened
3 cups confectioners' sugar
1 teaspoon vanilla extract

1. Preheat the oven to 350 degrees. Coat a 9x13-inch baking pan with non-stick cooking spray. In a large mixing bowl, beat the eggs, sugar, brown sugar and oil for 1 minute. Beat in the applesauce.

2. Sift the flour, cinnamon, cloves, baking powder and salt over the bowl and beat on low speed until the flour disappears. Gently fold in the carrots and walnuts or raisins. Pour and spread the batter into the pan. Bake for 35-40 minutes or until a toothpick comes out dry when inserted in the center of the cake. Frost after the cake has cooled.

3. To make the frosting, beat the softened cream cheese and butter for 1 minute. Add the confectioners' sugar and vanilla and beat until smooth and creamy. (Add more sugar if frosting is not thick enough.) Keep the cake cool until ready to serve.

<u>Tomato Soup Cake with Cinnamon-Cream Cheese Frosting</u>

This fun cake tastes like carrot cake.

2 eggs
1—10.75 oz. can condensed tomato soup (low sodium)
1 cup sugar
1/3 cup brown sugar
½ cup canola or vegetable oil
1 teaspoon vanilla extract
1/3 cup milk
2 cups flour
2 teaspoons ground cinnamon
¼ teaspoon ground cloves
2 teaspoons baking powder
frosting-
1–8oz. package cream cheese, softened
¼ cup warm milk
½ teaspoon vanilla extract
2 cups confectioners' sugar
¼ teaspoon ground cinnamon

1. Preheat the oven to 350 degrees. Coat a 10-inch bundt or tube cake pan with non-stick cooking spray. In a large mixing bowl, whisk the eggs. Add the soup, sugar, brown sugar, oil, vanilla and milk and whisk until blended.

2. Sift the flour, cinnamon, cloves and baking powder over the bowl and gently whisk until the flour disappears. Pour the batter into the pan and bake for 30-35 minutes or until a toothpick comes out dry when inserted into the center of the cake. Cool for 10 minutes and then turn out of the pan to cool completely.

3. To make the frosting, beat the cream cheese, warm milk and vanilla until smooth. Add the confectioners' sugar and cinnamon and beat on low until the sugar disappears. Then beat on high speed for 1 minute. (It should be thick and spreadable. Add more sugar if too runny, more milk if too stiff.) Pour and spread evenly over the cooled cake.

Cinnamon-Banana-Chocolate Chip Coffee Cake

A tempting trio of flavors.

topping-
1/3 cup sugar
1/3 cup flour
1 teaspoon ground cinnamon
6 tablespoons butter, melted
½ cup semi-sweet chocolate chips
cake-
2 very ripe (brown spotted) bananas (about 2/3 cup)
2 eggs
½ cup sugar
½ cup canola or vegetable oil
1/3 cup milk
1 teaspoon vanilla extract
1-1/3 cups flour
1 teaspoon ground cinnamon
1 teaspoon baking powder
½ teaspoon salt

1. Preheat the oven to 350 degrees. Coat an 8-inch square or 9-inch round baking pan with non-stick cooking spray. To make the topping, whisk the sugar, flour and cinnamon in a medium bowl. Stir in the melted butter, then stir in the chocolate chips and set aside.

2. In a large mixing bowl, mash the bananas. Whisk in the eggs. Add the sugar, oil, milk and vanilla and whisk until blended. Sift the flour, cinnamon, baking powder and salt over the bowl and gently whisk until the flour disappears (the batter will be lumpy).

3. Pour and spread the batter into the pan, sprinkle with the topping, and bake for 30-35 minutes or until the cake turns brown and a toothpick comes out dry when inserted into the center.

No-Bake Easter Egg Hunt Cake

Kids of all ages can hunt for the hidden candy poked inside.

1-10 oz. pound cake
15-20 jelly beans, robin eggs or small chocolate eggs (unwrapped)
2 cups whipped cream topping
1 cup cherry or strawberry pie filling
1/3 cup flaked coconut
colorful Easter candy (Peeps, Robin Eggs, chocolate bunnies, etc.)

1.   Line the bottom of an 8-inch square pan or ceramic dish with half-inch thick slices of pound cake. Press candy pieces into the slices of cake throughout the pan.

2.   Slowly and gently fold the whipped cream into the pie filling until evenly blended. Pour and spread the whipped cream mixture over the cake. Sprinkle with the flaked coconut.

3.   Decorate the top with colorful Easter candy. Refrigerate until ready to serve.

Cinnamon Sugar Loaf

A simple and satisfying treat.

topping-
2 teaspoons ground cinnamon
1/3 cup sugar
cake-
3 eggs
¾ cup canola or vegetable oil
¾ cup sugar
2 teaspoons vanilla extract
¾ cup milk
2 cups flour
1 ½ teaspoons baking powder
½ teaspoon salt

1. Preheat the oven to 350 degrees. Coat a 9x5-inch loaf pan with non-stick cooking spray. Stir together the cinnamon and sugar and set aside.

2. In a large mixing bowl, whisk the eggs. Add the oil, sugar, vanilla and milk and whisk until blended. Sift the flour, baking powder and salt over the bowl and gently whisk until the batter is smooth.

3. Pour half of the batter into the pan. Sprinkle with half of the cinnamon-sugar mixture. Pour the remaining batter into the pan and sprinkle with the rest of the topping. Bake for 40-50 minutes or until a toothpick comes out dry when inserted into the center. Sprinkle the top with an additional teaspoon of sugar. Let the pan cool for 10 minutes. Then remove the cake from pan and place on a rack to cool completely.

Lemon Sugar-Crusted Poppy Seed Loaf

Glistening lemon sugar graces this classic cake.

lemon sugar-
2 tablespoons sugar
2 drops lemon extract
cake-
3 eggs
1 cup sugar
¾ cup canola or vegetable oil
¾ cup milk
¼ cup poppy seeds
1 teaspoon vanilla extract
1 teaspoon lemon extract
1 ¾ cups flour
1 ½ teaspoons baking powder
½ teaspoon salt

1. Preheat the oven to 350 degrees. Coat a 9x5-inch loaf pan with non-stick cooking spray. To make the lemon sugar, use a fork or small whisk to mix the lemon extract into the sugar. Set aside.

2. In a large mixing bowl, whisk the eggs. Add the sugar, oil, milk, poppy seeds and extracts and whisk until blended. Sift the flour, baking powder and salt over the bowl and gently whisk until the flour disappears (the batter will be lumpy).

3. Pour the batter into the pan and sprinkle the top with the lemon sugar. Bake for 45-50 minutes or until a toothpick comes out dry when inserted into the center. Sprinkle an additional teaspoon of sugar over the warm cake. Let the pan cool for 10 minutes. Then remove the cake from pan and place on a rack to cool completely.

Lemon Buttermilk Pound Cake

Fresh, cool flavors in a luscious pound cake.

3 eggs
1 ¼ cups sugar
½ cup (1 stick) butter, melted
1 teaspoon lemon extract
1 teaspoon vanilla extract
1 cup buttermilk
2 cups flour
1 ½ teaspoons baking powder
½ teaspoon salt (omit if using salted butter)
lemon glaze-
1 cup confectioners' sugar
5 teaspoons warm milk
1/8 teaspoon lemon extract

1. Preheat the oven to 350 degrees. Coat a 9x5-inch loaf pan with non-stick cooking spray. In a large mixing bowl, whisk the eggs. Add the sugar, melted butter, extracts and buttermilk and whisk until blended. Sift the flour, baking powder and salt over the bowl and gently whisk until the flour disappears.

2. Pour the batter into the pan and bake for 45-50 minutes or until the cake turns brown and a toothpick comes out dry when inserted into the center. Cool for 10 minutes then remove the cake from the pan to cool completely. Top with lemon glaze.

3. To make the glaze, whisk the confectioners' sugar, milk and lemon extract together until smooth (add more sugar if too runny, more milk if too stiff). Drizzle over the cake.

Cream & Sugar Sheet Cake with Butter-Almond Glaze

Cream and sugar are for more than just coffee.

3 eggs
1 cup cream or "half & half"
¾ cup sugar
1 teaspoon vanilla extract
1 ¾ cups flour
1 ½ teaspoons baking powder
½ teaspoon salt
glaze-
1 cup sugar
½ cup (1 stick) butter, melted
¼ cup cream or "half & half"
1 teaspoon vanilla extract
1 cup sliced almond pieces

1. Preheat the oven to 350 degrees. Coat a 12x18-inch baking sheet with a 1-inch rim with non-stick cooking spray. In a large mixing bowl, whisk the eggs. Whisk in the cream, sugar and vanilla. Sift the flour, baking powder and salt over the bowl and gently whisk until blended.

2. Pour and spread the batter evenly into the pan. Bake for 10 minutes or until the cake is firm but not yet brown. While the cake is baking, prepare the glaze.

3. Whisk the sugar, butter, cream and vanilla until smooth. After removing the cake from the oven, turn the heat up to 400 degrees. Spread the glaze over the baked cake, sprinkle the top with the almond pieces, and set back in the oven until the topping is bubbling and begins to brown around the edges (about 5 minutes).

Quick Cookies

Classic Chocolate Chip Cookies

Not too thin and not too thick, these chocolate chip cookies are just right.

1 cup (2 sticks) butter, softened
1 cup sugar
½ cup brown sugar
2 eggs
1 teaspoon vanilla extract
2 ½ cups flour
½ teaspoon baking soda
1 teaspoon salt (omit if using salted butter)
2 cups semi-sweet chocolate chips

1. Preheat the oven to 375 degrees. In a large mixing bowl, beat the butter, sugar and brown sugar for half a minute. Add the eggs and vanilla and beat until smooth.

2. Add <u>1 cup</u> of the flour, the baking soda and salt to the batter and beat until smooth. Add the remaining one and one-half cups of flour and beat on low speed until the batter is once again smooth. Stir in the chocolate chips.

3. Set tablespoonfuls of the batter 2-inches apart onto cookie sheets and bake for 8-10 minutes or until the cookies are brown around the edges and begin to turn brown on top. Makes about 3 dozen cookies.

Chocolate-Chocolate-Chocolate Cookies

What could be better?

¾ cup (1 ½ sticks) butter, softened
¾ cup brown sugar
½ cup sugar
2 eggs
1 teaspoon vanilla extract
1 ¾ cups flour
¼ cup unsweetened cocoa powder
½ teaspoon baking soda
½ teaspoon salt (omit if using salted butter)
2 cups semi-sweet chocolate chips
topping:
2 teaspoons unsweetened cocoa powder
2 tablespoons sugar

1. Preheat the oven to 375 degrees. In a large mixing bowl, beat the butter, brown sugar and sugar for half a minute. Add the eggs and vanilla and beat until smooth.

2. Add 1 cup of the flour, the cocoa powder, baking soda and salt to the bowl and beat until smooth. Add the remaining ¾ cup of flour and beat again until smooth. Stir in the chocolate chips.

3. Set tablespoonfuls of the batter 2-inches apart onto cookie sheets and bake for 8-10 minutes or until the cookies are set on top (are no longer wet). Make the topping by blending the cocoa powder with the sugar. While the cookies are still warm, dip the tops into the cocoa-sugar mix. Makes about 3 dozen cookies.

Chocolate Cranberry Cookies

Sweet-tart cranberries are decadent surrounded in chocolate.

1 cup (2 sticks) butter, softened
1 cup brown sugar
½ cup sugar
2 eggs
1 teaspoon vanilla extract
2 cups flour
½ cup unsweetened cocoa powder
½ teaspoon baking soda
1 teaspoon salt (omit if using salted butter)
1-1/3 cups semi-sweet chocolate chips
1 cup dried cranberries

1. Preheat the oven to 375 degrees. In a large mixing bowl, beat the butter, brown sugar and sugar for half a minute. Add the eggs and vanilla and beat until smooth.

2. Add 1 cup of the flour, the cocoa powder, baking soda and salt and beat until the mixture is smooth. Add the remaining cup of flour and beat on low until blended. Stir in the chocolate chips and cranberries.

3. Set tablespoonfuls of the batter 2-inches apart onto cookie sheets and bake for 8-10 minutes or until the cookies have set in the center (no longer wet). Makes about 3 dozen cookies.

Chocolate-Kissed Candy Cane Cookies

Put holiday candy canes to yummy use in this fun recipe.

¾ cup (1 ½ sticks) butter, softened
2/3 cup sugar
1 egg
1 teaspoon vanilla extract
2 cups flour
1 teaspoon baking soda
½ teaspoon salt (omit if using salted butter)
½ cup crushed candy canes (about 7 standard size canes)
35-40 Hershey's Kisses
extra sugar for coating cookies

1. Preheat the oven to 375 degrees. In a large mixing bowl, beat the butter and sugar for half a minute. Beat in the egg and vanilla. Add 1 cup of the flour, the baking soda and salt to the bowl and beat until smooth. Add the remaining cup of flour and the candy canes and beat on low speed until well combined.

2. Roll the batter into 1 ½-inch balls and roll each ball into a small dish of sugar. Set the balls 2-inches apart onto cookie sheets and bake for 8-10 minutes or until the cookies turn brown on the bottom, not on top. (Use a butter knife or spatula to peek underneath.)

3. As soon as the cookies come out of the oven, press a chocolate kiss into the center of each. (Kisses will soften and then harden again.) Cookies are ready when the chocolate has set. Makes about 3 dozen cookies.

Black & Whites

Double your pleasure with the taste of dark and white chocolate.

1 cup (2 sticks) butter, softened
1 cup brown sugar
½ cup sugar
2 eggs
1 teaspoon vanilla extract
2 ¼ cups flour
½ cup unsweetened cocoa powder
½ teaspoon baking soda
1 teaspoon salt (omit if using salted butter)
1 cup white chocolate chips
1 cup semi-sweet chocolate chips

1. Preheat the oven to 375 degrees. In a large mixing bowl, beat the butter, brown sugar and sugar for half a minute. Beat in the eggs and vanilla.

2. Add <u>1 cup</u> of the flour, the cocoa powder, baking soda and salt to the batter and beat until smooth and creamy. Add the remaining 1 ¼ cups flour and beat on low speed until blended. Stir in the chocolate chips.

3. Set tablespoonfuls of the batter 2-inches apart onto cookie sheets and bake for 8-10 minutes or until the cookies are set in the center (no longer wet). Makes about 3 dozen cookies.

<u>Chocolate Charms</u>

A divine, melt in your mouth chocolate experience!

1 ¼ cups good quality semi-sweet chocolate chips
4 ounces (half a block package) cream cheese, softened
1 cup confectioners' sugar
1 teaspoon vanilla extract

1. Melt the chocolate chips. Set aside to cool.

2. Beat the cream cheese for half a minute. Add the confectioners' sugar and vanilla and beat on high speed for half a minute. Pour the melted chocolate (be sure that it is no longer hot) into the bowl and beat on low speed until the mixture is well blended. Cover the bowl and refrigerate for a minimum of 30 minutes.

3. When you are ready, scoop out the chocolate with a spoon and roll into 1-inch balls. Roll the balls into chopped nuts, colored sugar, candy or sprinkles, if desired. Makes about 25 pieces.

Lemon Sugar Topped Cookies

Simply sweet and delicious!

½ cup (1 stick) butter, softened
¾ cup sugar
1 egg
1 teaspoon vanilla extract
1 teaspoon lemon extract
1 ¼ cups flour
½ teaspoon baking soda
½ teaspoon salt (omit if using salted butter)
lemon sugar-
¼ cup sugar
¼ teaspoon lemon extract

1. Preheat the oven to 375 degrees. In a large mixing bowl, beat the butter and sugar for half a minute. Beat in the egg and the extracts. Add one-quarter cup of the flour, the baking soda and salt to the bowl and beat until smooth. Beat in the remaining cup of flour.

2. Drop heaping teaspoonfuls of batter onto cookie sheets, setting them 2-inches apart. To make the lemon sugar, whisk together the sugar and lemon extract.

3. Press the bottom of a smooth-bottomed glass into the lemon-sugar and press each cookie down to one-quarter inch thickness. (Dip the glass into the sugar after each press.) Bake for 7-9 minutes or until the cookies turn brown around the edges. Press the tops of the cookies into the remaining lemon-sugar while they are warm. Makes about 3 dozen cookies.

Cinnamon Oatmeal Cookies

Applesauce and brown sugar make these soft cookies wholesomely delectable.

1 cup brown sugar
½ cup sugar
½ cup (1 stick) butter, softened
2 eggs
1 teaspoon vanilla extract
¾ cup applesauce
1 ½ cups flour
1 teaspoon ground cinnamon
½ teaspoon baking soda
½ teaspoon salt (omit if using salted butter)
1 ¾ cups oats
1 cup raisins
1 cup chopped walnuts

1.   Preheat the oven to 375 degrees. In a large mixing bowl, beat the brown sugar, sugar and butter for half a minute. Add the eggs, vanilla and applesauce and beat until well blended.

2.   Add 1 cup of the flour, the cinnamon, baking soda and salt to the bowl and beat until smooth. Add the remaining half-cup of flour and oats and beat again until smooth. Stir in the raisins and walnuts.

3.   Set tablespoonfuls of the batter 2-inches apart onto cookie sheets. Bake for 8-10 minutes or until the cookies turn brown around the edges and begin to turn brown on top. Makes 3 dozen cookies.

Team Spirit Sugar Cookies

In Chicago we make these blue and orange.

¾ cup (1 ½ sticks) butter, softened
1 cup sugar
1 egg
2 teaspoons vanilla extract
2 cups flour
½ teaspoon baking soda
¾ teaspoon salt (omit if using salted butter)
colored sugar (team colors)

1. Preheat the oven to 375 degrees. In a large mixing bowl, beat the butter and sugar for half a minute. Beat in the egg and vanilla. Add 1 cup of the flour, the baking soda and salt to the bowl and beat until smooth. Add the remaining cup of flour and beat again until smooth.

2. Drop heaping teaspoonfuls of the batter 2-inches apart onto cookie sheets. Place one of the colored sugars into a small, shallow bowl. Dip a flat bottomed glass moistened with a bit of the batter into the sugar and press down each cookie to about one-quarter inch thickness. (Dip the glass into the sugar after each press.) Then sprinkle each cookie with the other color of sugar.

3. Bake for 7-10 minutes or until the cookies begin to turn brown around the edges.

Slice n' Bake Sugar Cookies

Make batter now, bake cookies later!

1 cup (2 sticks) butter, softened
1½ cups sugar
2 eggs
2 teaspoons vanilla extract
3 cups flour
1 teaspoon baking soda
1 teaspoon salt (omit if using salted butter)

1. In a large mixing bowl, beat the butter and sugar for half a minute. Beat in the eggs and vanilla. Add <u>1 cup</u> of the flour, the baking soda and salt and beat until the batter is smooth. Add the remaining 2 cups of flour and beat again until the batter is smooth.

2. Set one-third of the dough on a piece of waxed or parchment paper (large enough to wrap the dough in) and shape it into a cylinder about 2-inches in diameter. Roll and cover the dough with the paper (you can roll it like play-dough to make the cylinder smooth). Repeat with the two remaining piece of dough. Wrap each cylinder in aluminum foil and store in the refrigerator for up to 5 days or the freezer for up to 3 months.

3. Preheat the oven to 375 degrees. Unwrap the dough, cut into quarter-inch slices and set each slice 1-inch apart on cookie sheets. Top with candy sprinkles or colored sugar, or frost and decorate after the cookies have baked. Bake for 7-10 minutes or until the cookies begin to turn brown around the edges. Makes about 4 dozen cookies.

Vanilla Pudding-Chocolate Chip Cookies

Pudding mix makes these cookies soft and sweet.

1 cup (2 sticks) butter, softened
½ cup sugar
½ cup brown sugar
2 eggs
2 ¼ cups flour
1 package (3.4 ounce) instant vanilla pudding mix
½ teaspoon baking soda
½ teaspoon salt (omit if using salted butter)
2 cups semi-sweet chocolate chips

1. Preheat the oven to 375 degrees. In a large mixing bowl, beat the butter, sugar and brown sugar for half a minute. Add the eggs and beat until blended.

2. Add <u>1 cup</u> of the flour, the pudding mix, baking soda and salt to the bowl and beat until smooth. Add the remaining 1 ¼ cups of flour and beat again until smooth. Stir in the chocolate chips.

3. Set tablespoonfuls of the batter 2-inches apart onto cookie sheets. Bake for 8-10 minutes or until the cookies are brown around the edges and begin to turn brown on top. Makes about 3 dozen cookies.

Ranger Cookies

Full of wholesome flavor and crunch.

1 cup (2 sticks) butter, softened
1 cup sugar
1 cup brown sugar
2 eggs
2 teaspoons vanilla extract
2 cups flour
1 teaspoon baking soda
1 teaspoon salt (omit if using salted butter)
2 cups oats
1 cup shredded coconut
2 cups crisped rice cereal (like Rice Krispies)
1 cup semi-sweet chocolate chips
1 cup butterscotch chips
½ cup chopped walnuts

1. Preheat the oven to 375 degrees. In a large mixing bowl, beat the butter, sugar and brown sugar for half a minute. Beat in the eggs and vanilla.

2. Add 1 cup of the flour, the baking soda and salt to the bowl and beat until the batter is smooth. Add the remaining cup of flour, oats and coconut and beat until well combined. Stir in the rice cereal, chocolate chips, butterscotch chips and walnuts.

3. Set tablespoonfuls of the batter 2-inches apart onto cookie sheets. Bake for 8-10 minutes or until the cookies turn brown around the edges and begin to turn brown on the top. Makes about 3 dozen.

Peanut Butter-Oatmeal-Chocolate Chip Cookies

A delectable trio.

¾ cup (1 ½ sticks) butter, softened
1 cup peanut butter
1 cup sugar
½ cup brown sugar
2 eggs
2 cups flour
1 teaspoon baking soda
½ teaspoon salt (omit if using salted butter)
1 ½ cups oats
1 ½ cups semi-sweet chocolate chips
½ cup chopped peanuts (optional)

1. Preheat the oven to 375 degrees. In a large mixing bowl, beat the butter, peanut butter, sugar and brown sugar for half a minute. Beat in the eggs.

2. Add 1 cup of the flour, the baking soda and salt to the bowl and beat until smooth. Add the remaining cup of flour and the oats and beat again until well blended. Stir in the chocolate chips, and peanuts if using.

3. Set tablespoonfuls of the batter 2-inches apart onto cookie sheets. Bake for 8-10 minutes or until the cookies turn brown around the edges and begin to turn brown on top. Makes about 3 dozen cookies.

Potato Chip Cookies

A salty—sweet sensation!

1 cup (2 sticks) butter, softened
1 ½ cups sugar
2 eggs
1 teaspoon vanilla extract
2 ½ cups flour
½ teaspoon baking soda
2 cups crushed potato chips
1 ½ cups vanilla or white chocolate flavored chips

1. Preheat the oven to 375 degrees. In a large mixing bowl, beat the butter and sugar for half a minute. Beat in the eggs and vanilla.

2. Add <u>1 cup</u> of the flour and baking soda to the bowl and beat until the batter is smooth. Add the remaining 1 ½ cups of flour and beat again until smooth. Stir in the potato chips and butterscotch morsels.

3. Set tablespoonfuls of the batter 2-inches apart onto cookie sheets. Bake for 8-10 minutes or until the cookies turn brown around the edges and begin to turn brown on top. Makes about 3 dozen cookies.

Pumpkin Bread-Chocolate Chip Cookies

The best of both worlds in a soft, scrumptious cookie

6 tablespoons butter, softened
1 cup sugar
2 eggs
1 teaspoon vanilla extract
1 cup canned pumpkin
2 cups flour
1 teaspoon ground cinnamon
½ teaspoon baking soda
½ teaspoon salt
1 cup semi-sweet chocolate chips
1 cup chopped walnuts
topping-
¼ cup sugar
½ teaspoon ground cinnamon

1. Preheat the oven to 375 degrees. In a large mixing bowl, beat the butter and sugar for half a minute. Add the eggs, vanilla and pumpkin and beat until smooth.

2. Add <u>1 cup</u> of the flour, the cinnamon, baking soda and salt to the bowl and beat until smooth. Pour in the remaining cup of flour and beat again until smooth. Stir in the chocolate chips and walnuts.

3. Set tablespoonfuls of the batter 2-inches apart onto cookie sheets and bake for 8-10 minutes or until the cookies turn brown around the edges and begin to turn brown on top. Mix the sugar and cinnamon together. Dip the tops of the warm cookies into the mixture. Makes about 3 dozen cookies.

Power Cookies

These cookies give you the energy you need to get through the day.

¾ cup (1 ½ sticks) butter, softened
¾ cup sugar
½ cup brown sugar
2 eggs
1 teaspoon vanilla extract
2 cups flour
½ teaspoon baking soda
½ teaspoon salt (omit if using salted butter)
1 cup oats
1 cup granola or muesli cereal
1 cup semi-sweet chocolate chips

1. Preheat the oven to 375 degrees. In a large mixing bowl, beat the butter, sugar and brown sugar for half a minute. Beat in the eggs and vanilla.

2. Add 1 cup of the flour, the baking soda and salt and beat until the batter is smooth. Add the remaining cup of flour and the oats and beat again until smooth. Stir in the cereal and chocolate chips.

3. Set tablespoonfuls of batter 2-inches apart onto cookie sheets. Bake for 8-10 minutes or until the cookies are brown around the edges and begin to turn brown on top. Makes about 3 dozen cookies.

Maple Glazed Oatmeal Cookies

The crisp sugar-maple glaze is a tantalizing finish to this chewy cookie!

¾ cup (1 ½ sticks) butter, softened
¼ cup maple syrup
1 cup sugar
1 teaspoon vanilla extract
1 egg
1 ¾ cups flour
1 teaspoon ground cinnamon
½ teaspoon baking soda
½ teaspoon salt (omit if using salted butter)
1 ½ cups oats
½ cup chopped walnuts
1 cup vanilla or white chocolate chips
additional sugar and maple syrup for cookie glaze (about a half cup of each)

1. Preheat the oven to 375 degrees. In a large mixing bowl, beat the butter, syrup, sugar and vanilla for half a minute. Beat in the egg.

2. Add 1 cup of the flour, the cinnamon, baking soda and salt and beat until the batter is smooth. Add the remaining ¾ cup of flour and the oats and beat again until smooth. Stir in the walnuts and chips.

3. Set tablespoonfuls of the batter 2-inches apart onto cookie sheets. Bake for 8-10 minutes or until the cookies turn brown around the edges and begin to turn brown on top. To make the glaze, pour one-half cup of sugar and one-half cup of maple syrup into separate small bowls. When the cookies have cooled off, dip the tops into the syrup, then into the sugar. Makes about 3 dozen cookies.

<u>Gingersnaps</u>

Who can forget these spunky childhood favorites?

¾ cup (1 ½ sticks) butter, softened
½ cup sugar
½ cup brown sugar
¼ cup molasses
2 eggs
2 teaspoons vanilla extract
2 ¼ cups flour
1 teaspoon ground cinnamon
1 teaspoon ground ginger
½ teaspoon ground cloves
1 teaspoon baking soda
½ teaspoon salt (omit if using salted butter)

1. Preheat the oven to 375 degrees. In a large mixing bowl, beat the butter, sugar, brown sugar and molasses for half a minute. Beat in the eggs and vanilla.

2. Add <u>1 cup</u> of the flour, the cinnamon, ginger, cloves, baking soda and salt to the bowl and beat until the batter is smooth. Add the remaining 1 ¼ cups of flour and beat again until smooth.

3. Set tablespoonfuls of batter 2-inches apart onto cookie sheets. Flatten each cookie to one-quarter inch thickness using a flat-bottomed glass dipped in sugar. (Dip the glass into the sugar before flattening each cookie.) Bake for 8-10 minutes or until the cookies turn brown around the edges. Makes about 3 dozen cookies.

Butterscotch Cookies

These cookies are like a big butterscotch hug.

1 cup (2 sticks) butter, softened
1 cup brown sugar
¼ cup sugar
2 eggs
1 teaspoon vanilla extract
2-1/3 cups flour
½ teaspoon baking soda
½ teaspoon salt (omit if using salted butter)
1 ½ cups butterscotch morsels
½ cup chopped pecans (optional)

1.   Preheat the oven to 375 degrees. In a large mixing bowl, beat the butter, brown sugar and sugar for half a minute. Beat in the eggs and vanilla.

2.   Add <u>1 cup</u> of the flour, the baking soda and salt to the bowl and beat until the batter is smooth. Add the remaining 1-1/3 cups of flour and beat again until smooth. Stir in the butterscotch morsels, and pecans if using.

3.   Set tablespoonfuls of batter 2-inches apart onto cookie sheets. Bake for 8-10 minutes or until cookies turn brown around the edges and begin to turn brown on top. Makes about 3 dozen cookies.

Snickerdoodles

No one can resist this charming American cookie.

1 cup (2 sticks) butter, softened
1 ½ cups sugar
2 eggs
1 teaspoon vanilla extract
2-2/3 cups flour
2 teaspoons cream of tartar
½ teaspoon baking soda
½ teaspoon salt (omit if using salted butter)
coating-
2 teaspoons ground cinnamon
3 tablespoons sugar

1. Preheat the oven to 375 degrees. In a large mixing bowl, beat the butter and sugar for half a minute. Beat in the eggs and vanilla.

2. Add <u>1 cup</u> of the flour, the cream of tartar, baking soda and salt to the bowl and beat until the batter is smooth. Add the remaining 1-2/3 cups of flour and beat again until smooth.

3. Mix the cinnamon and sugar together to make the coating. Roll the batter into 1 ½-inch balls and roll each ball in the cinnamon-sugar. Set 2-inches apart onto cookie sheets and bake for 8-10 minutes or until the cookies are puffed up and brown around the edges. Makes about 3 dozen cookies.

Coo-Coo Cookies

Go crazy and stir your favorite cereal and flavored chips into these fun cookies.

2 cups unsweetened grain cereal (corn flakes, bran flakes, Wheaties, Chex …)
1 cup (2 sticks) butter, softened
1 cup sugar
½ cup brown sugar
2 eggs
1 teaspoon vanilla
2 cups flour
½ teaspoon baking soda
½ teaspoon salt (omit if using salted butter)
1 cup oats
1 ½ cups any flavor chips (chocolate, white chocolate, butterscotch, peanut butter …)

1. Preheat the oven to 375 degrees. Pour the cereal into a plastic bag and use your fingers or a mallet to crush it into small crumbs. Set aside.

2. In a large mixing bowl, beat the butter, sugar and brown sugar for half a minute. Beat in the eggs and vanilla. Add 1 cup of the flour, the baking soda and salt to the bowl and beat until the batter is smooth. Add the remaining cup of flour and the oats and beat again until smooth. Stir in the flavored chips and cereal.

3. Set tablespoonfuls of the batter 2-inches apart onto cookie sheets. Bake for 8-10 minutes or until the cookies turn brown around the edges and begin to turn brown on top. Makes about 3 dozen cookies.

Figgy Cookies

Who needs figgy pudding when you can have cookies.

½ cup (1 stick) butter, softened
½ cup sugar
¼ cup brown sugar
1 egg
1 teaspoon vanilla or rum extract
1 ¼ cups flour
1 teaspoon ground cinnamon
¼ teaspoon ground cloves
½ teaspoon baking soda
¼ teaspoon salt (omit if using salted butter)
1 cup dried figs, chopped into quarter-inch pieces
1 cup chopped walnuts

1. Preheat the oven to 350 degrees. In a large mixing bowl, beat the butter, sugar and brown sugar for half a minute. Beat in the egg and extract.

2. Add ¼ cup of the flour, the cinnamon, cloves, baking soda and salt and beat until the batter is smooth. Add the remaining cup flour and beat again until smooth. Stir in the figs and nuts.

3. Set heaping teaspoonfuls of batter 2-inches apart onto cookie sheets. Bake for 10-12 minutes or until the cookies turn brown around the edges. Makes about 2 dozen cookies.

Chocolate-Kissed Peanut Butter Cookies

Chocolate kisses nestled into sugared peanut butter cookies.

½ cup (1 stick) butter, softened
¾ cup peanut butter
½ cup sugar
1/3 cup brown sugar
1 egg
1 ½ cups flour
½ teaspoon baking soda
½ teaspoon salt (omit if using salted butter)
additional sugar for coating
1–8 ounce bag Hershey's Kisses (about 30 kisses), unwrapped

1. Preheat the oven to 350 degrees. In a large mixing bowl, beat the butter, peanut butter, sugar and brown sugar for half a minute. Beat in the egg.

2. Add 1 cup of the flour, the baking soda and salt to the bowl and beat until the batter is smooth. Add the remaining half-cup of flour and beat again until smooth.

3. Roll the batter into 1-inch balls, roll in sugar to coat, and set 2-inches apart onto cookie sheets. Bake for 8-10 minutes or until the cookies turn brown on the bottom, not on top. (Use a butter knife or spatula to lift and check underneath.) Press a chocolate kiss into the center of each cookie as soon as they come out of the oven. Makes about 3 dozen cookies.

Beehive Cookies

A cookie with a sweet sting of honey.

2/3 cup honey
½ cup sugar
½ cup (1 stick) butter, softened
1 egg
2 teaspoons vanilla extract
2 cups flour
1 teaspoon ground cinnamon
½ teaspoon baking soda
¼ teaspoon salt
additional sugar for topping

1. Preheat the oven to 375 degrees. In a large mixing bowl, beat the honey, sugar and butter for half a minute. Beat in the egg and vanilla.

2. Add 1 cup of the flour, the cinnamon, baking soda and salt to the bowl and beat until the batter is smooth. Add the remaining cup of flour and beat again until smooth.

3. Set tablespoonfuls of the batter 2-inches apart onto cookie sheets. Bake for 8-10 minutes or until the cookies turn brown around the edges and begin to turn brown on top. Dip the tops of the cookies in additional sugar while they are still warm.

Spice Cookies

Sugar and spice are oh-so nice in this tasty cookie.

1 cup (2 sticks) butter, softened
1 ½ cups sugar
2 eggs
2 teaspoons vanilla extract
2 ½ cups flour
1 teaspoon ground cinnamon
½ teaspoon ground nutmeg
¼ teaspoon ground cloves
½ teaspoon baking soda
½ teaspoon salt (omit if using salted butter)
topping-
¼ cup sugar
1 teaspoon ground cinnamon

1. Preheat the oven to 375 degrees. In a large mixing bowl, beat the butter and sugar for half a minute. Beat in the eggs and vanilla.

2. Add 1 cup of the flour, the spices, baking soda and salt and beat until the batter is smooth. Add the remaining 1 ½ cups of flour and beat again until smooth.

3. Roll the batter into 1 ½-inch balls and set 3-inches apart onto a cookie sheet. Blend the sugar and cinnamon together in a shallow dish. Dip the bottom of a flat-bottomed glass into the cinnamon sugar and press each ball to one-quarter inch thickness. (Press the glass into the cinnamon-sugar between each cookie.) Bake for 8-10 minutes or until the cookies turn brown around the edges. Makes about 4 dozen cookies.

Breakfast Cookies

A tasty way to get through the morning.

1 cup (2 sticks) butter, softened
¾ cup sugar
½ cup brown sugar
2 eggs
1 teaspoon vanilla extract
1 ¾ cups flour
1 teaspoon ground cinnamon
½ teaspoon baking soda
½ teaspoon salt (omit if using salted butter)
1 cup oats
2 cups corn flakes
1 cup chopped walnuts

1. Preheat the oven to 375 degrees. In a large mixing bowl, beat the butter, sugar and brown sugar for half a minute. Beat in the eggs and vanilla.

2. Add <u>1 cup</u> of the flour, the cinnamon, baking soda and salt to the bowl and beat until the batter is smooth. Add the remaining ¾ cup of flour and the oats and beat again until smooth. Stir in the corn flakes and walnuts.

3. Set tablespoonfuls of the batter 2-inches apart onto cookie sheets. Bake for 8-10 minutes or until the cookies turn brown around the edges and begin to turn brown on top. Makes about 3 dozen cookies.

Triple-Tasty Oatmeal Cookies

A wholesome and delicious trio of flavors.

1 cup (2 sticks) butter, softened
1 cup sugar
½ cup brown sugar
2 eggs
1 teaspoon vanilla extract
1 ¾ cups flour
1 teaspoon ground cinnamon
½ teaspoon baking soda
½ teaspoon salt (omit if using salted butter)
2 cups oats
1-1/3 cups semi-sweet chocolate chips
1 cup chopped walnuts

1. Preheat the oven to 375 degrees. In a large mixing bowl, beat the butter, sugar and brown sugar for half a minute. Beat in the eggs and the vanilla.

2. Add the <u>1 cup</u> of the flour, cinnamon, baking soda and salt and beat until the batter is smooth. Beat in the remaining ¾ cup of flour and oats. Stir in the chocolate chips and walnuts.

3. Set tablespoonfuls of the batter 2-inches apart onto cookie sheets. Bake for 8-10 minutes or until the cookies turn brown around the edges and begin to turn brown on top. Makes about 3 dozen cookies.

Vanilla Pecan Cookies

Luxurious flavors in a simple cookie.

1 cup (2 sticks) butter, softened
1 cup sugar
½ cup brown sugar
2 eggs
1 teaspoon vanilla extract
2 ½ cups flour
1 teaspoon ground cinnamon
½ teaspoon baking soda
½ teaspoon salt (omit if using salted butter)
1 ½ cups vanilla or white chocolate chips
1 cup chopped pecans

1. Preheat the oven to 375 degrees. In a large mixing bowl, beat the butter, sugar and brown sugar for half a minute. Beat in the eggs and vanilla.

2. Add 1 cup of the flour, the cinnamon, baking soda and salt and beat until smooth. Add the remaining 1 ½ cups of flour and beat again until smooth. Stir in the chips and pecans.

3. Set tablespoonfuls of the batter 2-inches apart onto cookie sheets. Bake for 8-10 minutes or until the cookies turn brown around the edges and begin to turn brown on top. Makes about 3 dozen cookies.

Iced Oatmeal Spice Cookies

A chewy cookie with a shiny, melt in your mouth icing.

10 tablespoons (1 stick plus 2 tablespoons) butter, softened
½ cup sugar
¼ cup brown sugar
1 egg
1 teaspoon vanilla extract
1 cup flour
½ teaspoon baking soda
½ teaspoon salt (omit if using salted butter)
1 teaspoon ground cinnamon
¼ teaspoon ground cloves
1 ½ cups oats
½ cup raisins, chopped into small bits
icing-
2 cups confectioners' sugar
1 tablespoon light corn syrup
¼ cup warm milk

1. Preheat the oven to 375 degrees. In a large mixing bowl, beat the butter, sugar and brown sugar for half a minute. Beat in the egg and vanilla. Add the flour, baking soda and salt and beat until the batter is smooth. Add the oats and chopped raisins and beat once more until blended.

2. Set tablespoonfuls of the batter 2-inches apart onto cookie sheets. Bake for 8-10 minutes or until the cookies turn brown around the edges and begin to turn brown on top.

3. To make the icing, blend the confectioners' sugar, the corn syrup and warm milk with a whisk until smooth. (Add more milk if too stiff, more sugar if too runny.) When the cookies have cooled off, dip the tops of the cookies into the icing. Makes about 2 dozen cookies.

Chocolate Toffee Bar Cookies

This cookie is more like chewy-chocolate candy.

4 ounces (1 long package) Saltine crackers
1 cup (2 sticks) butter
1 cup brown sugar
1 ½ cups semisweet chocolate chips

1. Preheat the oven to 400 degrees. Coat a 10x15-inch jellyroll pan with non-stick cooking spray or line with parchment paper. Cover the bottom of the pan with the crackers.

2. Melt the butter and brown sugar in a saucepan. Bring to a boil. Cook and stir over low heat for 2 minutes, then pour and spread the mixture over the crackers. Set the pan into the oven and bake for 5 minutes.

3. After baking, immediately sprinkle the top with the chocolate chips. Let the chips sit for about 5 minutes to melt, then spread with a spatula. Cut into squares when the chocolate has set. (Before the chocolate sets, sprinkle with chopped almonds or pecans, if desired.)

Almond Snow Crescents

Winter is not complete without making a batch of these.

1 cup (2 sticks) butter, softened
¼ cup sugar
¼ cup confectioners' sugar
1 teaspoon salt (omit if using salted butter)
2 cups flour
2 teaspoons vanilla extract
½ cup ground almonds
additional confectioners' sugar for coating

1. Preheat the oven to 350 degrees. In a large mixing bowl, beat the butter, sugar, confectioners' sugar and salt for half a minute. Add <u>1 cup</u> of the flour, the vanilla and ground almonds to the bowl and beat until the batter is smooth. Add the remaining cup of flour and beat again until a smooth dough forms.

2. Roll the dough into 1-inch balls and set 3-inches apart onto cookie sheets. Press each ball down to about one-half inch thickness and shape into a crescent. Bake for 10-12 minutes or until the bottoms (not the tops) of the cookies begin to turn brown. (Peek underneath a cookie with a butter knife to check.)

3. After the cookies have cooled for 5 minutes, roll them in confectioners' sugar. When the cookies have cooled completely, roll in confectioners' sugar again. Makes about 5 dozen cookies.

Coconut Macaroons

It doesn't get quicker, chewier or sweeter than this.

1—14 ounce bag (about 5 cups) sweetened flaked coconut
½ cup flour
1—14 ounce can sweetened condensed milk
2 teaspoons vanilla extract

1. Preheat the oven to 350 degrees. In a large mixing bowl, toss the coconut with the flour.

2. Add the condensed milk and vanilla and stir until mixture is well combined.

3. Spoon 1-inch dollops of the mixture onto cookie sheets, setting them 2-inches apart. Bake for 8-10 minutes or until the cookies begin to turn brown.

Lord Licorice Cookies

Just the smell of these cookies will send you back to Candyland.

½ cup (1 stick) butter, softened
¾ cup sugar
1 egg
2 teaspoons anise extract
1 teaspoon vanilla extract
1 ½ cups flour
¼ teaspoon baking soda
½ teaspoon salt (omit if using salted butter)
red or black licorice candy (about 30 pieces)
extra sugar for coating

1. Preheat the oven to 375 degrees. In a large mixing bowl, beat the butter and sugar for half a minute. Beat in the egg, anise and vanilla extracts. Add ½ cup of the flour, the baking soda and salt to the bowl and beat until the batter is smooth. Add the remaining cup of flour and beat again until smooth.

2. Roll the dough into 1-inch balls, roll the balls in sugar, and set them 2-inches apart onto cookie sheets. Bake for 8-10 minutes or until the cookies begin to turn brown around the edges.

3. While the cookies are still warm, press a licorice candy into the center of each. Makes about 2 dozen cookies.

Mini-Muffin Tea Cookies

Cute bite-sized cookies topped with your favorite fruit jam.

½ cup (1 stick) butter, softened
1/3 cup sugar
1 egg yolk
1 teaspoon vanilla extract
1 ¼ cups flour
¼ teaspoon salt (omit if using salted butter)
fruit jam for topping

1. Preheat the oven to 350 degrees. Coat a 24 cup mini-muffin pan with non-stick cooking spray. In a large mixing bowl, beat the butter and sugar for half a minute. Beat in the egg yolk and vanilla. Add the flour and salt to the bowl and beat until the batter is well combined and crumbly.

2. Shape the dough into one-inch balls and set into the muffin cups. Press each ball down making a well in the center for the jam.

3. Spoon one-half teaspoon of jam into each cup. Bake for 12-15 minutes or until the cookies begin to turn brown around the edges. Sprinkle with confectioner's sugar, if desired.

Lollypop Cookies

These are great to make with kids or to give as gifts.

¾ cup (1 ½ sticks) butter, softened
1 ¼ cups sugar
2 eggs
1 teaspoon vanilla extract
2 ½ cups flour
1 teaspoon baking soda
½ teaspoon salt (omit if using salted butter)
20 lollypop sticks

1. Preheat the oven to 350 degrees. In a large mixing bowl, beat the butter and sugar for half a minute. Beat in the eggs and vanilla. Add <u>1 cup</u> of the flour, the baking soda and salt and beat until the batter is smooth. Add the remaining 1 ½ cups of flour and beat again until smooth.

2. Shape the dough into large 2-inch balls and set 3-inches apart onto cookie sheets. Poke a stick into the center of the side of each ball (the stick should be parallel to the cookie sheet). Press each ball down to one-half inch thickness with a wide, flat-bottomed glass dipped in sugar. (Dip the glass into the sugar between each cookie.)

3. Decorate with colorful sprinkles, sugars or small pieces of candy like M&M's. (Or, bake them plain and frost and decorate after they have cooled.) Bake for 12-15 minutes or until the cookies turn brown around the edges. Makes about 20 cookie-pops.

Snowball Cookies (a.k.a. Russian Tea Cakes)

These traditional cookies will take you back to Christmas past.

1 cup (2 sticks) butter, softened
½ cup confectioners' sugar
2 cups flour
1 teaspoon vanilla extract
½ teaspoon salt (omit if using salted butter)
¾ cup finely chopped walnuts or pecans
additional confectioners' sugar for coating

1. Preheat the oven to 350 degrees. Beat the butter and sugar for half a minute. Add 1 cup of the flour, the vanilla and salt and beat until smooth. Add the remaining cup of flour and the nuts and beat again until a smooth dough forms.

2. Roll the dough into 1-inch balls and set 2-inches apart onto cookie sheets. Bake for 10-12 minutes or until the bottoms of the cookies turn brown. (Don't let the tops turn brown. Simply use a butter knife to lift and peek underneath a cookie to check.)

3. While the cookies are warm, roll them into a small dish of confectioners' sugar. When the cookies have cooled completely, roll in the sugar once again. Makes about 4 dozen cookies.

No-Bake Picnic Cookies

This version includes brown sugar, peanut butter and crispy cereal.

1 cup sugar
1 cup brown sugar
4 tablespoons unsweetened cocoa powder
½ cup (1 stick) butter
½ cup milk
1 cup peanut butter
2 teaspoons vanilla extract
2 cups quick cooking oats
2 cups crisped rice cereal

1. In a large cooking pot, whisk the sugar, brown sugar and cocoa powder until blended. Cut the butter into 5 or 6 pieces and toss into the pan, along with the milk.

2. Place the pot over medium-high heat and stir until the mixture comes to a full boil. Reduce the heat to low and let it boil for 2 minutes without stirring.

3. Remove the pan from the heat and stir in the peanut butter and vanilla. Then stir in the oats and cereal. Drop heaping teaspoonfuls of the mixture onto wax or parchment paper so cookies can cool and set. Makes about 4 dozen.

Cookie Pizza

Making this recipe is almost as much fun as eating it.

dough-
10 tablespoons (1 stick plus 2 tablespoons) butter, softened
¾ cup sugar
1 egg
1 ½ cups flour
½ teaspoon baking soda
top-
1—8 ounce package cream cheese
1 ½ cups Marshmallow Fluff
red food coloring
1 cup shredded coconut
topping suggestions—chocolate, butterscotch, peanut butter or vanilla flavored chips, chopped nuts, small candy pieces like M&M's or crushed Heath bars, strawberries, blueberries or other pieces of fresh fruit, mini marshmallows, etc.

1. Preheat the oven to 375 degrees. Coat a 14-inch pizza pan or a 10x15-inch cookie sheet with non-stick cooking spray, or line with parchment paper. In a large mixing bowl beat the butter and sugar for half a minute. Beat in the egg.

2. Add ½ cup of the flour and the baking soda to the bowl and beat until the batter is smooth. Add the remaining cup of the flour to the bowl and beat until a smooth dough forms. Pour and spread the dough out onto the prepared pan. (It should be about one-half inch thick.) Bake for 10 minutes or until the top begins to turn brown.

3. To make the top, beat the cream cheese and marshmallow for half a minute. Add the food coloring to the desired shade of red. Spread evenly over the baked cookie base and sprinkle with toppings. Top with the shredded coconut and refrigerate until ready to serve.

On the Spot Brownies, Bars and Squares

Super One-Bowl Brownies

If you like yours extra fudgy or cakey, follow the tips below!

3 eggs
¾ cup sugar
½ cup brown sugar
¾ cup (1 ½ sticks) butter, melted
1 teaspoon vanilla extract
½ cup flour
¾ cup unsweetened cocoa powder
½ teaspoon salt (omit if using salted butter)
1 cup semi-sweet chocolate chips
½ cup chopped walnuts (optional)

1. Preheat the oven to 350 degrees. Coat an 8-inch square baking pan with non-stick cooking spray. In a large mixing bowl, whisk the eggs. Add the sugar, brown sugar, melted butter and vanilla and whisk until blended.

2. Sift the flour, cocoa powder and salt over the bowl and whisk until the batter is smooth. Stir in the chocolate chips, and nuts if using.

3. Pour the batter into the pan and bake for 25-30 minutes or until a toothpick comes out dry and crumbly when inserted <u>between</u> the edge and the center of the brownies.

* For fudgy brownies—reduce the flour by 2 tablespoons
* For cakey brownies—increase the flour by 2 tablespoons

Glazed Coffee Liqueur Brownies

If you like Kahlua, you'll love these.

3 eggs
1 ¼ cups sugar
½ cup (1 stick) butter, melted
¼ cup coffee flavored liqueur, like Kahlua
1 teaspoon vanilla extract
2/3 cup flour
½ cup unsweetened cocoa powder
¼ teaspoon salt (omit if using salted butter)
½ cup semi-sweet chocolate chips
glaze-
1 cup semi-sweet chocolate chips
1/3 cup coffee flavored liqueur
4 tablespoons butter

1. Preheat the oven to 350 degrees. Coat an 8-inch square baking pan with non-stick cooking spray. In a large mixing bowl, whisk the eggs. Add the sugar, melted butter, liqueur and vanilla and whisk until well blended.

2. Sift the flour, cocoa powder and salt over the bowl and whisk until the batter is smooth. Stir in the chocolate chips. Pour and spread the batter into the pan and bake for 25-30 minutes or until a toothpick comes out dry and crumbly when inserted <u>between</u> the center and the edge of the pan.

3. To make the glaze, combine the chocolate chips, liqueur and butter in a saucepan over medium heat and stir until melted. Pour and spread over the brownies.

Butterscotch Blondies

Butterscotch with a rich brownie texture.

2 eggs
¾ cup brown sugar
½ cup (1 stick) butter, melted
1 ½ teaspoons vanilla extract
1 ¼ cups flour
¼ teaspoon baking soda
½ teaspoon salt (omit if using salted butter)
1 cup butterscotch chips

1. Preheat the oven to 350 degrees. Coat an 8-inch square baking pan with non-stick cooking spray. In a large mixing bowl, whisk the eggs. Add the brown sugar, melted butter and vanilla and whisk until blended.

2. Sift the flour, baking soda and salt over the bowl and whisk until smooth. Stir in the chips.

3. Pour and spread the batter into the pan. Bake for 20-25 minutes or until edges turn brown and a toothpick comes out dry and crumbly when inserted into the center.

Rocky Road Brownies

Let rich chocolate, soft marshmallows and crunchy nuts take you on a tasty ride.

1 cup semi-sweet chocolate chips
½ cup (1 stick) butter
½ cup sugar
½ cup brown sugar
1 teaspoon vanilla extract
¼ teaspoon salt (omit if using salted butter)
2 eggs
2/3 cup flour
1 cup miniature marshmallows
1 cup chopped pecans, almonds or walnuts
additional ½ cup semi-sweet chocolate chips

1. Preheat the oven to 350 degrees. Coat an 8-inch square baking pan with non-stick cooking spray. Melt the chocolate and butter together. Pour into a mixing bowl, add the sugar, brown sugar, vanilla and salt and whisk until smooth. Whisk in the eggs until well blended.

2. Add the flour and whisk until the batter is smooth. Stir in the marshmallows, chopped nuts and chocolate chips.

3. Pour and spread the batter into the pan. Bake for 20-25 minutes or until a toothpick comes out dry and crumbly when inserted <u>between</u> the center and the edge of the pan.

Coffee Blondies

Make these when a cup of coffee just isn't enough.

3 eggs
1 cup brown sugar
½ cup sugar
1 cup (2 sticks) butter, melted
2 teaspoons vanilla extract
2 tablespoons instant coffee or espresso powder
¼ cup warm milk
2 cups flour
¼ teaspoon baking soda
½ teaspoon salt (omit if using salted butter)
2 cups vanilla or white chocolate chips

1. Preheat the oven to 350 degrees. Coat a 9x13-inch baking pan with non-stick cooking spray. In a large mixing bowl, whisk the eggs. Add the brown sugar, sugar, melted butter and vanilla and whisk until blended.

2. Stir the coffee powder into the warm milk and whisk it into the batter. Sift the flour, baking soda and salt over the bowl and whisk until the batter is smooth. Stir in the chips.

3. Pour and spread the batter into the pan and bake for 25-30 minutes or until the top turns brown and a toothpick comes out dry and crumbly when inserted into the center.

Chocolate Mint Brownies

Mint extract gives chocolate a decadent spark of flavor.

3 eggs
2/3 cup sugar
½ cup brown sugar
¾ cup (1 ½ sticks) butter, melted
1 teaspoon vanilla extract
½ teaspoon mint extract
2/3 cup flour
¾ cup unsweetened cocoa powder
½ teaspoon salt (omit if using salted butter)
1 cup semi-sweet chocolate chips
topping-
4 tablespoons (half a stick) butter
½ cup semisweet chocolate chips
1 cup confectioners' sugar
½ teaspoon mint extract

1. Preheat the oven to 350 degrees. Coat an 8-inch square baking pan with non-stick cooking spray. In a large mixing bowl, whisk the eggs. Add the sugar, brown sugar, melted butter, and extracts and whisk until blended.

2. Sift the flour, cocoa powder and salt over the bowl and whisk until the batter is smooth. Stir in the chocolate chips. Pour and spread the batter into the pan and bake for 25-30 minutes or until a toothpick comes out dry and crumbly when inserted <u>between</u> the edge and the center of the brownies.

3. To make the topping, melt the butter and chocolate. Add the confectioners' sugar and mint extract and whisk until smooth and creamy. Pour and spread over the brownies.

Chocolate Pecan Caramel Bars

Sweet, chewy pleasure.

35 caramel squares
¼ cup milk
1 cup flour
1 cup oats
½ cup sugar
¼ teaspoon baking soda
½ teaspoon salt (omit if using salted butter)
¾ cup (1 ½ sticks) butter, melted
1 cup semi-sweet chocolate chips
¾ cup chopped pecans

1. Preheat the oven to 350 degrees. Coat a 9x13-inch baking pan with non-stick cooking spray. In a saucepan over low heat, melt the caramels into the milk, stirring every few minutes until smooth.

2. While the caramels are melting, whisk together the flour, oats sugar, baking soda and salt in a large mixing bowl. Add the melted butter and stir until the mixture is well combined and crumbly. Press two-thirds of the mixture evenly into the bottom of the pan. Bake for 8-10 minutes or until the top begins to turn brown.

3. Stir the chocolate chips and pecans into the remaining oat mixture. Pour and spread the melted caramel over the baked bottom. Sprinkle the chocolate chip-nut mixture over the top and bake for 10-15 minutes or until the top turns light brown.

Simple S'more Bars

When a campfire and roasting sticks aren't around, try this recipe.

3 cups graham cracker crumbs
2/3 cup sugar
¾ cup (1 ½ sticks) butter, melted
3 cups mini-marshmallows
2 cups semi-sweet chocolate chips

1. Preheat the oven to 350 degrees. Coat a 9x13-inch baking pan with non-stick cooking spray. In a large mixing bowl, stir together the graham cracker crumbs, sugar and melted butter.

2. Pour two-thirds of the mixture into the pan and press down evenly on the bottom. Pour and spread the marshmallows over the mixture, then sprinkle with the chocolate chips. Sprinkle the remaining crumb mixture over the top and gently press down on all of the ingredients with a large spatula.

3. Bake for 10-15 minutes or until the marshmallows start to turn brown. Cut into squares and serve warm.

Power Bars

Full of flavor and energy.

2 eggs
½ cup honey
4 tablespoons (half a stick) butter, melted
1 cup peanut butter
½ cup brown sugar
2 teaspoons vanilla extract
1 cup flour
2 ½ cups oats
1 ½ cups toasted oat cereal, like Cheerios
½ cup nuts
½ cup raisins or other dried fruit
1 cup chocolate chips

1. Preheat the oven to 350 degrees. Coat a 9x13-inch baking pan with non-stick cooking spray. In a large mixing bowl, whisk the eggs. Add the honey, melted butter, peanut butter, brown sugar and vanilla and whisk until blended.

2. Add the flour and stir until the batter is smooth and well combined. Stir in the oats, cereal, nuts, raisins and chocolate chips.

3. Pour and spread the mixture into the pan. Bake for 20-25 minutes or until the top turns brown and a toothpick comes out dry and crumbly when inserted into the center.

Coconut Cookie Bars

A chewy cookie treat.

1 cup (2 sticks) butter, softened
½ cup sugar
½ cup brown sugar
1 egg
1 teaspoon vanilla extract
2 ¼ cups flour
½ teaspoon baking soda
½ teaspoon salt (omit if using salted butter)
1—14 ounce can sweetened condensed milk
2 eggs
2 cups flaked coconut

1. Preheat the oven to 350 degrees. Coat a 9x13-inch baking pan with non-stick cooking spray. In a large mixing bowl, beat the butter, sugar and brown sugar for half a minute. Beat in the egg and vanilla.

2. Sift the flour, baking soda and salt over the bowl and beat until the batter is smooth. Press evenly into the bottom of the pan and bake for 15 minutes.

3. Whisk together the condensed milk and the eggs until blended. Pour and spread over the baked cookie layer and sprinkle the coconut over the top. Bake for 15 minutes or until the top turns light brown.

Toasted Oat Cereal Bars

This fun, no-bake recipe is crisp and delicious!

3 tablespoons butter
1—10.5 ounce package mini-marshmallows
½ cup peanut butter, smooth or crunchy
5 cups Cheerios or other toasted oat cereal
1 cup M&M's or chocolate chips

1. Coat a 9x13-inch pan with non-stick cooking spray. In a large pot over medium heat, melt the butter. Add the marshmallows and stir until melted. Remove the pan from the heat.

2. Stir in the peanut butter. Add the cereal and additional ingredients and stir until everything is evenly coated with the marshmallow mixture.

3. Pour and spread into the pan. With buttered hands or a piece of waxed paper, press the mixture down firmly into the pan. Cut into squares when cool.

Frosted Vanilla Cookie Bars

Simple pleasure.

¾ cup (1 ½ sticks) butter, softened
1 cup sugar
1 egg
1 teaspoon vanilla extract
2 cups flour
¼ teaspoon baking soda
½ teaspoon salt (omit if using salted butter)
frosting-
2 cups confectioners' sugar
3 tablespoons butter, melted
2 tablespoons warm milk
1 teaspoon vanilla extract

1. Preheat the oven to 350 degrees. Coat a 9x13-inch baking pan with non-stick cooking spray. In a large mixing bowl, beat the butter and sugar for half a minute. Beat in the egg and vanilla. Add 1 cup of the flour, baking soda and salt and beat until the batter is smooth. Beat in the remaining cup of flour.

2. Pour and spread the batter into the pan. Bake for 20-25 minutes or until the top turns light brown and a toothpick comes out dry and crumbly when inserted into the center.

3. When the pan has cooled, beat all of the frosting ingredients together until smooth and creamy. (Add more confectioners' sugar if too runny, more milk if too stiff.) Spread evenly over the top.

Crisp Peanut Butter-Scotchies

No baking here—just quick, simple and sweet.

1 ½ cups butterscotch chips
2/3 cup peanut butter
4 ½ cups crisped rice cereal (like Rice Krispies)

1. Coat a 9x13-inch dish or baking pan with non-stick cooking spray. In a large pot over medium heat, stir the butterscotch chips and peanut butter until melted and smooth. Remove the pan from the heat.

2. Pour the cereal into the pan and stir gently until the cereal is coated with the mixture.

3. Pour and spread into the pan. Cut and serve when cool.

Chocolate Bar Peanut Butter Squares

Tasty peanut butter brownies under a firm chocolate topping.

½ cup (1 stick) butter, softened
½ cup sugar
½ cup brown sugar
½ cup peanut butter
2 eggs
1 teaspoon vanilla extract
1 ¼ cups flour
¼ teaspoon baking soda
¼ teaspoon salt (omit if using salted butter)
top-
1 ½ cups semi-sweet chocolate chips
¼ cup chopped peanuts (optional)

1. Preheat the oven to 350 degrees. Coat an 8-inch square baking pan with non-stick cooking spray. In a large mixing bowl, beat the butter, sugar, brown sugar and peanut butter for half a minute. Beat in the eggs and vanilla.

2. Sift the flour, baking soda and salt over the bowl and mix on low speed until the batter is smooth. Pour into the pan and bake for 25-30 minutes or until a toothpick comes out dry and crumbly when inserted into the center.

3. As soon as the pan comes out of the oven, sprinkle the chocolate chips over the top and let sit for about 5 minutes. Once the chocolate has softened, spread it evenly over the top. Sprinkle with chopped peanuts, if desired.

Toasted Almond Butter Cookie Squares

Cinnamon and brown-sugared almonds jazz up a spread of cookie dough.

top-
1–2 ounce bag sliced almonds (about 2/3 cup)
6 tablespoons butter
¼ cup brown sugar
1 teaspoon ground cinnamon
1/8 (a pinch) salt (omit if using salted butter)
1/3 cup flour
bottom-
½ cup (1 stick) butter, softened
¼ cup confectioners' sugar
½ cup sugar
1 egg
1 teaspoon vanilla extract
¼ teaspoon almond extract
1 cup flour
¼ teaspoon salt (omit if using salted butter)

1.   Preheat the oven to 350 degrees. Coat an 8-inch square baking pan with non-stick cooking spray. Spread the almonds in a skillet over medium heat, occasionally stirring until the almonds begin to turn brown.

2.   Remove the pan from the heat, add the butter and stir until melted. Stir in the brown sugar, cinnamon and salt. Then add the flour and stir until well combined and crumbly. Set aside.

3.   To make the bottom, beat the butter, confectioners' sugar and sugar for half a minute. Beat in the egg and extracts. Add the flour and salt and beat again until the batter is smooth. Pour and spread into the pan and sprinkle with the almond topping. Bake for 25-30 minutes or until the topping is lightly browned and a toothpick comes out dry when inserted into the center.

Pecan Squares

No time to make pecan pie? Try This.

bottom-
½ cup (1 stick) butter, softened
1/3 cup brown sugar
1 egg yolk (save the egg white for the top)
1 teaspoon vanilla extract
¼ teaspoon salt (omit if using salted butter)
1 cup flour
top-
1 egg white
1/3 cup brown sugar
1 teaspoon ground cinnamon
1 cup chopped pecans

1. Preheat the oven to 350 degrees. Coat an 8-inch square baking pan with non-stick cooking spray. Beat the butter and brown sugar for half a minute. Add the egg yolk, vanilla and salt and beat again until smooth.

2. Add the flour and beat on low speed until well combined. Pour and press the mixture evenly into the pan. Bake for 10-12 minutes or until it begins to turn brown around the edges.

3. To prepare the top, beat the egg white until frothy. Add the brown sugar and cinnamon and beat until the egg white begins to stiffen. Fold in the pecans. Pour and spread over the baked bottom layer. Bake for 15 minutes or until the top is light brown and firm to the touch.

Pumpkin Pie Brownie Squares

Rich brownies and spiced pumpkin are even better together.

bottom-
4 tablespoons (half a stick) butter
1/3 cup semi-sweet chocolate chips
1/3 cup sugar
1 egg
½ teaspoon vanilla extract
1/3 cup flour
1/8 teaspoon salt (omit if using salted butter)
top-
2 eggs
1–15 ounce can pumpkin
2/3 cup sugar
1 teaspoon ground cinnamon
1 ¼ cups evaporated milk

1. Melt the butter and chocolate and set aside to cool. Preheat the oven to 350 degrees. Coat an 8-inch square baking pan with non-stick cooking spray. Pour the melted chocolate into a mixing bowl and whisk in the sugar, egg and vanilla.

2. Add the flour and salt and whisk until the batter is smooth. Pour into the pan and bake for 12 minutes.

3. Increase the oven heat to 375 degrees. To make the top, whisk the eggs in a large mixing bowl. Add the pumpkin, sugar, cinnamon and evaporated milk and whisk until smooth. Pour over the brownie bottom and bake for 25 minutes or until the top is set and firm in the center. Serve each square with a dollop of whipped cream.

Groovy Peanut Butter-Chocolate Squares

The coolest way to put peanut butter and chocolate together.

2/3 cup peanut butter
4 tablespoons (half a stick) butter, softened
½ cup sugar
½ cup brown sugar
1 egg
1 teaspoon vanilla extract
1 cup flour
¼ teaspoon baking soda
1 ½ cups semi-sweet chocolate chips

1. Preheat the oven to 350 degrees. Coat an 8-inch square baking pan with non-stick cooking spray. In a large mixing bowl, beat the peanut butter, butter, sugar and brown sugar for half a minute. Beat in the egg and vanilla.

2. Sift the flour and baking soda over the bowl and mix on low speed until smooth. Pour and spread the batter into the pan and sprinkle the chocolate chips over the top.

3. Put the pan in the oven for 5 minutes. Then, with a butter knife or spatula, swirl the melted chocolate chips into the batter to create a marbleized look. Place the pan back into the oven and bake for 25-30 minutes or until brown around the edges and a toothpick comes out dry and crumbly when inserted between the center and the edge of the pan.

Nut *du Jour* Squares

Stir your favorite nuts into these snazzy cinnamon squares.

½ cup (1 stick) butter, softened
¼ cup sugar
½ cup brown sugar
2 eggs
1 teaspoon vanilla extract
1 cup flour
2 teaspoons ground cinnamon
¼ teaspoon baking soda
¼ teaspoon salt (omit if using salted butter)
1 cup chopped nuts (walnuts, pecans, cashews, almonds, peanuts …)
glaze-
½ cup confectioners' sugar
2 teaspoons warm milk

1. Preheat the oven to 350 degrees. Coat an 8-inch square baking pan with non-stick cooking spray. In a large mixing bowl, beat the butter, sugar and brown sugar for half a minute. Add the eggs and vanilla and beat again until smooth.

2. Sift the flour, cinnamon, baking soda and salt over the bowl and beat until smooth and creamy. Stir in the chopped nuts.

3. Pour and spread the batter into the pan. Bake for 25-30 minutes or until the top turns light brown and a toothpick comes out dry and crumbly when inserted into the center. When the pan is cool, whisk together the confectioners' sugar and warm milk and drizzle over the top.

Praline Crunch Squares

A cookie and candy baked into one cute bite.

1 box shortbread cookies
1 cup brown sugar
1 cup (2 sticks) butter
1 teaspoon vanilla extract
1 cup chopped pecans
½ teaspoon salt (omit if using salted butter)

1. Preheat the oven to 350 degrees. Cover a 15x12-inch cookie sheet with parchment paper or spray with non-stick cooking spray. Cover the bottom of the cookie sheet with 1 layer of shortbread cookies.

2. In a medium-sized saucepan, combine the brown sugar and butter and bring to a gentle boil over medium heat, stirring frequently. Boil gently (reducing the heat if necessary) for 2 minutes. Remove from heat and stir in the vanilla, pecans and salt.

3. Pour and spread the mixture evenly over the cookies and bake for 10 minutes. Cut into squares while still warm. Serve when the squares have cooled completely.

Marshmallow Mumbo-Jumbo Squares

Irresistible flavors packed into a cute, little square.

5 tablespoons butter, melted
1 ½ cups graham cracker crumbs
1 jar (7.5 oz.) Marshmallow Fluff
1/3 cup milk
1 cup semisweet chocolate chips
1 cup flaked coconut
1 cup chopped walnuts, pecans or almonds

1. Preheat the oven to 350 degrees. Pour and spread the melted butter into an 8-inch square baking pan. Sprinkle the cracker crumbs over the butter.

2. In a small saucepan, combine the fluff and milk and stir over medium heat until smooth. Pour evenly over the crumbs. Sprinkle the chocolate, coconut and walnuts over the top and press down gently.

3. Bake 25-30 minutes or until the marshmallow is lightly browned.

Crispy Chocolate-Topped Peanut Butter Fluff Squares

A party of fun flavors!

1–7 ½ ounce jar Marshmallow Fluff
2 tablespoons butter
½ cup peanut butter
1 cup dry roasted peanuts
3 cups crisped rice cereal (like Rice Krispies)
2 cups semisweet chocolate chips (divided)
1 (additional) tablespoon butter

1. Coat an 8-inch square baking pan with non-stick cooking spray. In a medium saucepan, melt the marshmallow and butter over medium heat. Remove the pan from the heat, add the peanut butter, and stir until smooth.

2. Add the peanuts, cereal and 1 cup of the chocolate chips to the fluff mixture and stir until every thing is well combined.

3. Pour and spread the mixture into the pan. Melt the remaining 1 cup chocolate chips with 1 tablespoon of butter. Pour and spread over the top.

Caramel Apple Squares

Just like eating a caramel apple, only better.

bottom-
1 cup flour
¼ cup brown sugar
1 teaspoon ground cinnamon
½ cup (1 stick) butter, melted
1/8 teaspoon salt (omit if using salted butter)
top-
¼ cup flour
½ cup brown sugar
2 large eggs
1 teaspoon vanilla extract
2 large apples, cored, and chopped into bite-sized pieces (about 2 cups)
1 cup caramels cut into pieces, (cut each square into 4 pieces)
½ cup chopped walnuts or pecans

1. Preheat the oven to 350 degrees. Coat an 8-inch square baking pan with non-stick cooking spray. Whisk the flour, brown sugar, and cinnamon together. Add the melted butter and salt and stir until well combined and crumbly. Pour and press down evenly into the pan. Bake for 12 minutes or until the top begins to turn brown.

2. To make the top, whisk together the flour and brown sugar. Whisk in the eggs and vanilla. Stir in the apple pieces, caramels and chopped nuts.

3. Pour and spread the apple mixture over the baked bottom. Bake for 25 minutes or until the top turns brown. When bars are still warm, cut into squares with a buttered knife.

Muffins and Scones in a Jiffy

Cinnamon Vanilla Chip Muffins

Brown sugar and cinnamon cuddle up deliciously in these muffins.

2 eggs
¾ cup sugar
2/3 cup canola or vegetable oil
¾ cup milk
1 teaspoon vanilla extract
1 ¾ cups flour
2 teaspoons baking powder
½ teaspoon salt
2/3 cup vanilla or white chocolate chips
topping-
¼ cup sugar
1 teaspoon ground cinnamon

1. Preheat the oven to 375 degrees. Coat a 12-cup muffin pan with non-stick cooking spray. In a large mixing bowl whisk the eggs. Add the sugar, oil, milk and vanilla and whisk until blended.

2. Sift the flour, baking powder and salt over the bowl and gently whisk until the flour disappears (the batter will be lumpy). Gently fold in the chips.

3. Use a quarter-cup scoop to spoon the batter into the muffin cups. Blend the sugar and cinnamon together and sprinkle 1 teaspoon of the mixture over each muffin. Bake for 18-20 minutes or until the muffins begin to turn brown and a toothpick comes out dry when inserted into the center.

Chocolate Chip Muffins

Chomp into one of these and you'll feel like a kid again!

2 eggs
½ cup sugar
2/3 cup canola or vegetable oil
¾ cup milk
1 teaspoon vanilla extract
1 ¾ cups flour
2 teaspoons baking powder
½ teaspoon salt
1 ¼ cups semi-sweet chocolate chips
topping-
2 tablespoons brown sugar
2 tablespoons sugar

1. Preheat the oven to 375 degrees. Coat a 12-cup muffin pan with non-stick cooking spray. In a large mixing bowl whisk the eggs. Add the sugar, oil, milk and vanilla and whisk until blended.

2. Sift the flour, baking powder and salt over the bowl and gently whisk until the flour disappears (the batter will be lumpy). Gently fold in the chocolate chips.

3. Use a quarter-cup measure to spoon the batter into the muffin cups. Mix the brown sugar with the sugar and sprinkle 1 teaspoon of the mixture over each cup. Bake for 18-20 minutes or until the muffins turn light brown and a toothpick comes out dry when inserted into the center.

Vanilla Orange Muffins

Smooth vanilla and perky orange are tasty fun together.

2 eggs
¾ cup sugar
2/3 cup canola or vegetable oil
¼ cup milk
½ cup fresh orange juice
1 tablespoon freshly grated orange peel
1 teaspoon vanilla extract
1 ¾ cups flour
1 ½ teaspoons baking powder
½ teaspoon salt
1 cup white chocolate or vanilla flavored chips
additional sugar for topping

1. Preheat the oven to 375 degrees. Coat a 12-cup muffin pan with non-stick cooking spray. In a large mixing bowl, whisk the eggs. Add the sugar, oil, milk, orange juice, orange peel and vanilla and whisk until blended.

2. Sift the flour, baking powder and salt over the bowl and gently whisk until the flour disappears (the batter will be lumpy). Gently fold in the chips.

3. Use a quarter-cup scoop to spoon the batter into the muffin cups. Sprinkle the top of each muffin with one-half teaspoon of sugar. Bake for 18-20 minutes or until muffins begin to turn brown and a toothpick comes out dry when inserted into the center.

Cinnamon-Sugared Applesauce Walnut Muffins

Sweet and crunchy fall flavors in every bite.

2 eggs
2/3 cup sugar
2/3 cup canola or vegetable oil
1 cup applesauce
1 teaspoon vanilla extract
2 cups flour
2 teaspoons ground cinnamon
2 teaspoons baking powder
½ teaspoon salt
1 cup chopped walnuts
topping-
2 tablespoons sugar
1 teaspoon ground cinnamon

1. Preheat the oven to 375 degrees. Coat a 12-cup muffin pan with non-stick cooking spray. In a large mixing bowl, whisk the eggs. Add the sugar, oil, applesauce and vanilla and whisk until blended.

2. Sift the flour, cinnamon, baking powder and salt over the bowl and gently whisk until the flour disappears (the batter will be lumpy). Gently fold in the walnuts.

3. Use a quarter-cup scoop to spoon the batter into the muffin cups. In a small bowl, stir together the sugar and cinnamon and sprinkle one-half teaspoon over each muffin. Bake for 18-20 minutes or until the muffins begin to turn brown and a toothpick comes out dry when inserted into the center.

Coffee Glazed Mocha Muffins

Cinnamon-chocolate muffins with rousing coffee flavor.

2 eggs
¾ cup sugar
2/3 cup canola or vegetable oil
2 tablespoons instant espresso or coffee powder
¾ cup warm milk
1 teaspoon vanilla extract
1 ¾ cups flour
1 teaspoon cinnamon
2 teaspoons baking powder
½ teaspoon salt
¾ cup semi-sweet chocolate chips
glaze-
1 teaspoon instant coffee or espresso powder
3 tablespoons warm milk or cream
1 ½ cups confectioners' sugar

1. Preheat the oven to 375 degrees. Coat a 12-cup muffin pan with non-stick cooking spray. In a large mixing bowl, whisk the eggs. Add the sugar, oil, coffee powder, warm milk and vanilla and whisk until blended.

2. Sift the flour, cinnamon, baking powder and salt over the bowl and gently whisk until the flour disappears (the batter will be lumpy). Fold in the chocolate chips. Use a quarter-cup scoop to spoon the batter into the muffin cups. Bake for 18-20 minutes or until the muffins begin to turn brown and a toothpick comes out dry when inserted in the center.

3. To make the glaze, blend the coffee powder into the warm milk until it dissolves. Add the confectioners' sugar and whisk until smooth. (Add more milk if too stiff, more sugar if too runny.) Drizzle over the tops of the muffins.

Glazed Eggnog Muffins

A sweet treat for the holidays.

2 eggs
¾ cup sugar
½ cup canola or vegetable oil
1 cup eggnog
1 teaspoon vanilla extract
1 ¾ cups flour
1 teaspoon ground nutmeg
1 teaspoon ground cinnamon
2 teaspoons baking powder
½ teaspoon salt
glaze-
2 cups confectioners' sugar
2 tablespoons melted butter
2 tablespoons eggnog
extra ground nutmeg for tops

1. Preheat the oven to 375 degrees. Coat a 12-cup muffin pan with non-stick cooking spray. In a large mixing bowl, whisk the eggs. Add the sugar, oil, eggnog and vanilla and whisk until blended. Sift the flour, nutmeg, cinnamon, baking powder and salt over the bowl and gently whisk until the flour disappears (the batter will be lumpy).

2. Use a quarter-cup scoop to spoon the batter into the muffin cups. Bake for 18-20 minutes or until the muffins begin to turn brown and a toothpick comes out dry when inserted into the center. Top each muffin with eggnog glaze and a small sprinkle of nutmeg.

3. To make the glaze, whisk the confectioners' sugar with the melted butter and eggnog. (Add more eggnog if too stiff, more sugar if too runny.)

Cinnamon Raisin Bran Muffins

Bran flakes give these muffins a nice, nutty flavor.

2 eggs
1 cup sugar
2/3 cup canola or vegetable oil
¾ cup milk
1 teaspoon vanilla extract
2 cups raisin bran cereal
1 ¼ cups flour
1 teaspoon ground cinnamon
2 teaspoons baking powder
½ teaspoon salt
topping-
¼ cup sugar
½ teaspoon ground cinnamon

1. Preheat the oven to 375 degrees. Coat a 12-cup muffin pan with non-stick cooking spray. In a large mixing bowl, whisk the eggs. Add the sugar, oil, milk and vanilla and whisk until smooth. Stir in the cereal.

2. Sift the flour, cinnamon, baking powder and salt over the bowl and gently stir until the flour disappears (the batter will be lumpy). Use a quarter-cup scoop to spoon the batter into the muffin cups.

3. Blend the sugar and cinnamon together and sprinkle 1-teaspoon of the mixture over each muffin. Bake for 18-20 minutes or until the muffins begin to turn brown and a toothpick comes out dry when inserted into the center.

Lemon Muffins

Pucker up and enjoy these refreshing muffins.

2 eggs
¾ cup sugar
2/3 cup canola or vegetable oil
¾ cup milk
1 teaspoon lemon extract
1 teaspoon vanilla extract
1 ¾ cups flour
2 teaspoons baking powder
½ teaspoon salt
glaze-
1 ½ cups confectioners' sugar
½ teaspoon lemon extract
2 tablespoons warm milk

1. Preheat the oven to 375 degrees. Coat a 12-cup muffin pan with non-stick cooking spray. In a large mixing bowl, whisk the eggs. Add the sugar, oil, milk and extracts and whisk until blended.

2. Sift the flour, baking powder and salt over the bowl and gently whisk until the flour disappears (the batter will be lumpy). Use a quarter-cup scoop to spoon the batter into the muffin cups. Bake for 18-20 minutes or until the muffins begin to turn brown and a toothpick comes out dry when inserted into the center.

3. To make the glaze, whisk the confectioners' sugar, lemon extract and warm milk until smooth (add more sugar if too runny, more milk if too stiff). Drizzle over the muffins.

Glazed Irish Cream Muffins

A delightful way to enjoy Irish cream liqueur.

2 eggs
¾ cup sugar
2/3 cup canola or vegetable oil
¼ cup Irish cream liqueur
1 tablespoon instant coffee powder
½ cup warm milk
1 ¾ cups flour
2 teaspoons baking powder
½ teaspoon salt
¾ cup white chocolate or vanilla flavored chips
glaze-
1 ½ cups confectioners' sugar
1 tablespoon Irish cream liqueur
2 tablespoons warm milk

1. Preheat the oven to 375 degrees. Coat a 12-cup muffin pan with non-stick cooking spray. In a large mixing bowl, whisk the eggs. Add the sugar, oil and liqueur and whisk until smooth. Dissolve the coffee powder into the warm milk, add to the batter, and whisk again until smooth.

2. Sift the flour, baking powder and salt over the bowl and gently whisk until the flour disappears (the batter will be lumpy). Gently fold in the chips.

3. Use a quarter-cup scoop to spoon the batter into the muffin cups. Bake for 18-20 minutes or until the muffins begin to turn brown and a toothpick comes out dry when inserted into the center. To make the glaze, whisk the confectioners' sugar, liqueur and warm milk until smooth. (Add more milk if too stiff, more sugar if too runny.) Drizzle over the muffins.

Sugared Applesauce Muffins

Applesauce makes these irresistibly moist and delicious.

2 eggs
¾ cup sugar
½ cup canola or vegetable oil
1 cup applesauce
1 teaspoon vanilla extract
2 cups flour
1 teaspoon ground cinnamon
2 teaspoons baking powder
½ teaspoon salt
1 apple, peeled, cored and cut into bite-sized bits (about 1 cup)
topping-
2 tablespoons sugar
2 tablespoons brown sugar
½ teaspoon ground cinnamon

1. Preheat the oven to 375 degrees. Coat a 12-cup muffin pan with non-stick cooking spray. In a large mixing bowl, whisk the eggs. Add the sugar, oil, applesauce and vanilla and whisk until blended.

2. Sift the flour, cinnamon, baking powder and salt over the bowl and gently whisk until the flour disappears (the batter will be lumpy). Fold in the apple pieces.

3. Use a quarter-cup scoop to spoon the batter into the muffin cups. Mix the sugar, brown sugar and cinnamon together and sprinkle 1 teaspoon of the mixture over each muffin. Bake for 18-20 minutes or until the muffins begin to turn brown and a toothpick comes out dry when inserted into the center.

Sour Cream Coffee Cake Muffins

Hand-held coffee cake ready to go when you are.

topping-
½ cup sugar
¼ cup flour
1 teaspoon ground cinnamon
6 tablespoons butter, melted
batter-
2 eggs
¾ cup sugar
½ cup canola or vegetable oil
1 cup sour cream
1 teaspoon vanilla extract
2 cups flour
2 teaspoons baking powder
½ teaspoon salt

1. Preheat the oven to 375 degrees. Coat a 12-cup muffin pan with non-stick cooking spray. To make the topping, whisk the sugar, flour and cinnamon until blended. Add the melted butter and stir until well combined and crumbly. Set aside.

2. In a large mixing bowl, whisk the eggs. Add the sugar, oil, sour cream and vanilla and whisk until blended. Sift the flour, baking powder and salt over the bowl and gently whisk until the flour disappears (the batter will be lumpy).

3. Use a quarter-cup measure to spoon the batter into the muffin cups. Sprinkle 1-tablespoon of the topping over each muffin, pressing it down into the batter just a little. Bake for 18-20 minutes or until the muffins begin to turn brown and a toothpick comes out dry when inserted into the center.

Sugar-Topped Jelly Belly Muffins

Fill these with your favorite flavor of jelly or jam.

2 eggs
½ cup sugar
2/3 cup canola or vegetable oil
¾ cup milk
1 teaspoon vanilla extract
1 ¾ cups flour
2 teaspoons baking powder
½ teaspoon salt
½ cup jelly, jam or preserves
topping-
4 tablespoons melted butter
¼ cup sugar

1. Preheat the oven to 375 degrees. Coat a 12-cup muffin pan with non-stick cooking spray. In a large mixing bowl, whisk the eggs. Add the sugar, oil, milk and vanilla and whisk until blended.

2. Sift the flour, baking powder and salt over the bowl and gently whisk until the flour disappears (the batter will be lumpy).

3. Use a quarter-cup measure to spoon the batter into the muffin cups. Make a well in the center and set 2 teaspoons of jelly into the middle of each muffin. Bake for 18-20 minutes or until the muffins begin to turn brown. After they have cooled off dip the tops of the muffins into the melted butter. Then roll into the sugar.

Brown Sugar Butterscotch Muffins

Full of warm, comforting flavor.

topping-
½ cup brown sugar
¼ cup flour
1 teaspoon ground cinnamon
5 tablespoons melted butter
batter-
2 eggs
½ cup sugar
¼ cup brown sugar
2/3 cup canola or vegetable oil
¾ cup milk
1 teaspoon vanilla extract
1 ¾ cups flour
2 teaspoons baking powder
½ teaspoon salt
1 cup butterscotch chips

1. Preheat the oven to 375 degrees. Coat a 12-cup muffin pan with non-stick cooking spray. To make the topping, whisk together the brown sugar, flour and cinnamon. Stir in the melted butter and set aside.

2. In a large mixing bowl, whisk the eggs. Add the sugar, brown sugar, oil, milk and vanilla and whisk until blended. Sift the flour, baking powder and salt over the bowl and gently whisk until the flour disappears (the batter will be lumpy). Gently fold in the butterscotch chips.

3. Use a quarter-cup scoop to spoon the batter into the muffin cups. Spoon about 2 teaspoons of the topping over each muffin. Bake for 18-20 minutes or until the muffins begin to turn brown and a toothpick comes out dry when inserted into the center.

Cappuccino Muffins

Enjoy the taste of coffee and vanilla in a muffin.

2 eggs
2/3 cup canola or vegetable oil
¾ cup sugar
1 teaspoon vanilla extract
3 tablespoons instant coffee or espresso powder
¾ cup warm milk
1 ¾ cups flour
2 teaspoons baking powder
½ teaspoon salt
1 ¼ cups white chocolate or vanilla flavored chips

1. Preheat the oven to 375 degrees. Coat a 12-cup muffin pan with non-stick cooking spray. In a large mixing bowl, whisk the eggs. Add the oil, sugar and vanilla and whisk until blended. Stir the coffee powder into the warm milk and whisk into the batter.

2. Sift the flour, baking powder and salt over the bowl and gently whisk until the flour disappears (the batter will be lumpy). Gently fold in the chips.

3. Use a quarter-cup measure to spoon the batter into the muffin cups. Bake for 18-20 minutes or until a toothpick comes out dry when inserted into the center.

Cinnamon-Glazed Blueberry Muffins

Colorful, cozy and delicious.

2 eggs
½ cup sugar
2/3 cup canola or vegetable oil
¾ cup milk
1 teaspoon vanilla extract
1 ¾ cups flour
2 teaspoons baking powder
½ teaspoon salt
1 ¼ cups blueberries tossed with 2 teaspoons flour
glaze-
2 cups confectioners' sugar
½ teaspoon ground cinnamon
2 tablespoons melted butter
2 tablespoons warm milk
½ teaspoon vanilla extract

1. Preheat the oven to 375 degrees. Coat a 12-cup muffin pan with non-stick cooking spray. In a large mixing bowl, whisk the eggs. Add the sugar, oil, milk and vanilla and whisk until blended. Sift the flour, baking powder and salt over the bowl and gently whisk until the flour disappears (the batter will be lumpy). Fold in the flour-coated blueberries.

2. Use a quarter-cup scoop to spoon the batter into the muffin cups. Bake for 18-20 minutes or until the muffins begin to turn brown and a toothpick comes out dry when inserted into the center.

3. To make the glaze, whisk the confectioners' sugar with the cinnamon. Add the melted butter, warm milk and vanilla and whisk until smooth. (It should have the consistency of thick syrup. Add more milk if too stiff, more sugar if too runny.) Dip the tops of the muffins into the glaze.

<u>Vanilla-Glazed Raspberry Muffins</u>

These muffins look as loveable as they taste.

2 eggs
¾ cup sugar
2/3 cup canola or vegetable oil
¾ cup milk
1 teaspoon vanilla extract
1 ¾ cups flour
2 teaspoons baking powder
½ teaspoon salt
1 ¼ cups raspberries tossed with 2 teaspoons flour
glaze-
2 cups confectioners' sugar
2 tablespoons melted butter
2 tablespoons warm milk
½ teaspoon vanilla extract

1. Preheat the oven to 375 degrees. Coat a 12-cup muffin pan with non-stick cooking spray. In a large mixing bowl, whisk the eggs. Add the sugar, oil, milk and vanilla and whisk until blended. Sift the flour, baking powder and salt over the bowl and gently whisk until the flour disappears (the batter will be lumpy). Fold in the flour-coated raspberries.

2. Use a quarter-cup scoop to spoon the batter into the muffin cups. Bake for 18-20 minutes or until the muffins begin to turn brown and a toothpick comes out dry when inserted into the center.

3. To make the glaze, whisk the confectioners' sugar, melted butter, warm milk and vanilla until smooth. (It should have the consistency of thick syrup. Add more milk if too stiff, more sugar if too runny.) Dip the tops of the muffins into the glaze.

Fresh Strawberry Muffins

A scrumptious spring and summertime treat.

2 eggs
¾ cup sugar
2/3 cup canola or vegetable oil
¾ cup milk
1 teaspoon vanilla extract
1 ¾ cups flour
2 teaspoons baking powder
½ teaspoon salt
1 cup fresh strawberries cut into bite-sized bits
¼ cup (additional) sugar for topping

1. Preheat the oven to 375 degrees. Coat a 12-cup muffin pan with non-stick cooking spray. In a large mixing bowl, whisk the eggs. Add the sugar, oil, milk and vanilla and whisk until blended.

2. Sift the flour, baking powder and salt over the bowl and gently whisk until the flour disappears (the batter will be lumpy). Gently fold in the strawberries.

3. Use a quarter-cup scoop to spoon the batter into the muffin cups. Sprinkle 1-teaspoon of sugar over each muffin. Bake for 18-20 minutes or until the muffins begin to turn brown and a toothpick comes out dry when inserted into the center.

Upside-Down Honey Nut Muffins

A muffin with a sweet twist!

topping-
½ teaspoon ground cinnamon
½ cup brown sugar
2 tablespoons honey
2 tablespoons melted butter
¼ teaspoon vanilla extract
¾ cup chopped walnuts
batter-
1 egg
2/3 cup sugar
½ cup canola or vegetable oil
¾ cup milk
1 teaspoon vanilla extract
1 ¾ cups flour
1 ½ teaspoons baking powder
½ teaspoon salt

1. Preheat the oven to 375 degrees. Coat a 12-cup muffin pan with non-stick cooking spray. To make the topping, stir the cinnamon into the brown sugar. Add the honey, melted butter and vanilla and stir until well combined and crumbly. Stir in the nuts. Spoon this mixture into the bottom of the muffin cups.

2. To make the batter, whisk the egg in a large mixing bowl. Add the sugar, oil, milk and vanilla and whisk until blended. Sift the flour, baking powder and salt over the bowl and gently whisk until the flour disappears (the batter will be lumpy).

3. Use a quarter-cup scoop to spoon the batter into the muffin pan. Bake for 16-18 minutes or until the muffin tops begin to turn brown. Let the muffins sit for 5 minutes. Then turn them upside down and remove the muffin form. Spoon any honey mixture that might stick to the pan over the muffins.

Sugared Blueberry Muffins

A classic muffin topped with a sparkling sugar kiss.

2 eggs
¾ cup sugar
2/3 cup canola or vegetable oil
¾ cup milk
1 teaspoon vanilla extract
1 ¾ cups flour
2 teaspoons baking powder
½ teaspoon salt
1 ½ cups blueberries tossed with 1 tablespoon of flour
additional ¼ cup sugar for topping

1. Preheat the oven to 375 degrees. Coat a 12-cup muffin pan with non-stick cooking spray. In a large mixing bowl, whisk the eggs. Add the sugar, oil, milk and vanilla and whisk until blended.

2. Sift the flour, baking powder and salt over the bowl and gently whisk until the flour disappears (the batter will be lumpy.) Gently fold in the flour-coated blueberries.

3. Use a quarter-cup scoop to spoon the batter into the muffin cups. Top each with 1-teaspoon of sugar. Bake for 18-20 minutes or until the muffins begin to turn brown and a toothpick comes out dry when inserted into the center.

Sugared Banana Muffins

The best thing you can do with overripe bananas is mash them into muffin batter.

2 eggs
¾ cup sugar
½ cup canola or vegetable oil
½ cup milk
1 teaspoon vanilla extract
3 very ripe, brown-spotted bananas, mashed (about 1 cup)
2 cups flour
2 teaspoons baking powder
½ teaspoon salt
topping-
1 tablespoon brown sugar
2 tablespoons sugar
¼ teaspoon ground cinnamon

1. Preheat the oven to 375 degrees. Coat a 12-cup muffin pan with non-stick cooking spray. In a large mixing bowl, whisk the eggs. Add the sugar, oil, milk and vanilla and whisk until blended. Whisk in the mashed bananas.

2. Sift the flour, baking powder and salt over the bowl and gently whisk until the flour disappears (the batter will be lumpy). Use a quarter-cup scoop to spoon the batter into the muffin cups.

3. Blend the brown sugar, sugar and cinnamon together and sprinkle one-half teaspoon over each muffin. Bake for 18-20 minutes or until the muffins begin to turn brown and a toothpick comes out dry when inserted into the center.

Cinnamon-Kissed Pumpkin Muffins

This is topped with a shiny cinnamon glaze.

2 eggs
¾ cup sugar
½ cup canola or vegetable oil
1 ½ cups canned pumpkin
2 cups flour
1 teaspoon ground cinnamon
¼ teaspoon ground cloves
2 teaspoons baking powder
½ teaspoon salt
glaze-
2 cups confectioners' sugar
½ teaspoon ground cinnamon
3 tablespoons warm milk
½ teaspoon vanilla extract

1. Preheat the oven to 375 degrees. Coat a 12-cup muffin pan with non-stick cooking spray. In a large mixing bowl, whisk the eggs. Add the sugar, oil and pumpkin and whisk until blended. Sift the flour, cinnamon, cloves, baking powder and salt over the bowl and gently whisk until the flour disappears (the batter will be lumpy).

2. Use a quarter-cup scoop to spoon the batter into the muffin cups. Bake for 18-20 minutes or until the tops begin to turn brown and a toothpick comes out dry when inserted into the center.

3. To make the glaze, whisk the confectioners' sugar, cinnamon, warm milk and vanilla until smooth. (It should have the consistency of thick syrup. Add more milk if too stiff, more sugar if too runny.) Dip the tops of the muffins into the glaze.

Carrot Walnut Muffins

Healthful carrots and walnuts never tasted so good.

2 eggs
¾ cup sugar
2/3 cup canola or vegetable oil
2/3 cup milk
1 teaspoon vanilla extract
2 cups flour
2 teaspoons ground cinnamon
2 teaspoons baking powder
½ teaspoon salt
2 cups shredded carrots
¾ cup chopped walnuts
additional 2 tablespoons sugar for topping

1. Preheat the oven to 375 degrees. Coat a 12-cup muffin pan with non-stick cooking spray. In a large mixing bowl, whisk the eggs. Add the sugar, oil, milk and vanilla and whisk until blended.

2. Sift the flour, cinnamon, baking powder and salt over the bowl and gently whisk until the flour disappears (the batter will be lumpy). Gently fold in the carrots and walnuts.

3. Use a quarter-cup scoop to spoon the batter into the muffin cups. Sprinkle each with one-half teaspoon of sugar. Bake for 18-20 minutes or until the muffins begin to turn brown and a toothpick comes out dry when inserted into the center.

Cinnamon-Sugared Zucchini Muffins

You'll be amazed how good zucchini can taste.

2 eggs
¾ cup sugar
½ cup canola or vegetable oil
½ cup milk
1 teaspoon vanilla extract
2 cups flour
2 teaspoons ground cinnamon
2 teaspoons baking powder
½ teaspoon salt
1 cup grated zucchini
topping-
¼ cup sugar
½ teaspoon ground cinnamon

1. Preheat the oven to 375 degrees. Coat a 12-cup muffin pan with non-stick cooking spray. In a large mixing bowl, whisk the eggs. Add the sugar, oil, milk and vanilla and whisk until blended.

2. Sift the flour, cinnamon, baking powder and salt over the bowl and gently whisk until the flour disappears (the batter will be lumpy). Gently fold in the zucchini.

3. Use a quarter-cup scoop to spoon the batter into the muffin cups. Blend the sugar and cinnamon together and sprinkle 1-teaspoon over each muffin. Bake for 18-20 minutes or until the muffins begin to turn brown and a toothpick comes out dry when inserted into the center.

Pumpkin-Chocolate Chip Muffins

Rich and rustic.

2 eggs
¾ cup sugar
2/3 cup canola or vegetable oil
1 teaspoon vanilla extract
1 cup canned pumpkin
2 cups flour
1 teaspoon ground cinnamon
¼ teaspoon ground cloves
2 teaspoons baking powder
½ teaspoon salt
¾ cup semi-sweet chocolate chips
topping-
2 tablespoons sugar
½ teaspoon ground cinnamon

1. Preheat the oven to 375 degrees. Coat a 12-cup muffin pan with non-stick cooking spray. In a large mixing bowl, whisk the eggs. Add the sugar, oil and vanilla and whisk until blended. Add the pumpkin and whisk until the batter is smooth.

2. Sift the flour, cinnamon, cloves, baking powder and salt over the bowl and gently whisk until the flour disappears (the batter will be lumpy). Gently fold in the chocolate chips.

3. Use a quarter-cup scoop to spoon the batter into the muffin cups. Blend the sugar with the cinnamon and sprinkle one-half teaspoon of the mixture over each muffin. Bake for 18-20 minutes or until the muffins begin to turn brown and a toothpick comes out dry when inserted into the center.

Cinnamon-Pecan Sweet Potato Muffins

Sweet potatoes make these muffins wholesome, soft and satisfying.

2 eggs
¼ cup brown sugar
½ cup sugar
½ cup canola or vegetable oil
½ cup milk
1 teaspoon vanilla extract
1 cup mashed sweet potatoes
2 cups flour
2 teaspoons ground cinnamon
2 teaspoons baking powder
½ teaspoon salt
2/3 cup chopped pecans
topping-
2 tablespoons brown sugar
2 tablespoons sugar
½ teaspoon ground cinnamon

1. Preheat the oven to 375 degrees. Coat a 12-cup muffin pan with non-stick cooking spray. In a large mixing bowl, whisk the eggs. Add the brown sugar, sugar, oil, milk and vanilla and whisk until blended. Whisk in the sweet potatoes.

2. Sift the flour, cinnamon, baking powder and salt over the bowl and gently whisk until the flour disappears (the batter will be lumpy). Gently fold in the pecans.

3. Use a quarter-cup scoop to spoon the batter into the muffin cups. In a small bowl, blend the brown sugar, sugar and cinnamon. Sprinkle 1-teaspoon of the mixture over each muffin. Bake for 18-20 minutes or until the muffins begin to turn brown and a toothpick comes out dry when inserted into the center.

Banana-Walnut-Chocolate Chip Muffins

Every bite is crunchy sweet and delicious.

2 eggs
2/3 cup sugar
½ cup canola or vegetable oil
¼ cup milk
1 teaspoon vanilla extract
3 very ripe, brown spotted bananas, mashed (about 1 cup)
2 cups flour
2 teaspoons baking powder
½ teaspoon salt
2/3 cup semi-sweet chocolate chips
2/3 cup chopped walnuts
topping-
3 tablespoons sugar
2 tablespoons brown sugar
½ teaspoon ground cinnamon

1. Preheat the oven to 375 degrees. Coat a 12-cup muffin pan with non-stick cooking spray. In a large mixing bowl, whisk the eggs. Add the sugar, oil, milk and vanilla and whisk until blended. Whisk in the mashed bananas.

2. Sift the flour, baking powder and salt over the bowl and gently whisk until the flour disappears (the batter will be lumpy). Gently fold in the chocolate chips and walnuts.

3. Use a quarter-cup scoop to spoon the batter into the muffin cups. Blend the sugar, brown sugar and cinnamon together and sprinkle 1-teaspoon of the mixture over each muffin. Bake for 18-20 minutes or until the muffins begin to turn brown and a toothpick comes out dry when inserted into the center.

Quick Breads and Sweet Breakfasts

<u>Sugar-Buttered Gingerbread</u>

Spiced gingerbread glistening with buttery sweetness.

2 eggs
¾ cup sugar
¾ cup canola or vegetable oil
½ cup molasses
1-2/3 cups flour
2 teaspoons ground cinnamon
1 ½ teaspoons ground ginger
¼ teaspoon ground cloves
1 ½ teaspoons baking powder
½ teaspoon salt
2/3 cup soft raisins (optional)
topping-
3 tablespoons melted butter
2 tablespoons sugar

1. Preheat the oven to 350 degrees. Coat a 9x5-inch loaf pan with non-stick cooking spray. In a large mixing bowl, whisk the eggs. Add the sugar, oil and molasses and whisk until blended.

2. Sift the flour, cinnamon, ginger, cloves, baking powder and salt over the bowl and gently whisk until the flour disappears (the batter will be lumpy). Fold in the raisins if using.

3. Pour and spread the batter into the pan. Pour the melted butter over the top. Then sprinkle with <u>1 tablespoon</u> of sugar. Bake for 35-40 minutes or until a toothpick comes out dry when inserted into the center of the cake. Sprinkle the remaining tablespoon of sugar over the top.

Orange-Glazed Pumpkin Walnut Bread

A wholesome, sweet and delicious treat.

2 eggs
¾ cup sugar
1/3 cup canola or vegetable oil
½ cup milk
1 cup canned pumpkin
1 teaspoon vanilla extract
1-2/3 cups flour
1 teaspoon ground cinnamon
¼ teaspoon ground cloves
1 ½ teaspoons baking powder
½ teaspoon salt
¾ cup chopped walnuts
glaze-
1 cup confectioners' sugar
2 teaspoons warm orange juice

1. Preheat the oven to 350 degrees. Coat a 9x5-inch loaf pan with non-stick cooking spray. In a large mixing bowl, whisk the eggs. Add the sugar, oil, milk, pumpkin and vanilla and whisk until blended.

2. Sift the flour, cinnamon, cloves, baking powder and salt over the bowl and gently whisk until the flour disappears (the batter will be lumpy). Gently fold in the walnuts.

3. Pour and spread the batter into the pan. Bake for 35-40 minutes or until a toothpick comes out dry when inserted into the center. To make the glaze, whisk together the confectioners' sugar and orange juice until smooth and creamy. (Add more juice if too stiff, more sugar if too runny.) Pour over the cooled cake.

Cinnamon-Sugared Banana Bread

Cinnamon turns basic banana bread into a sumptuous treat.

3 very ripe (brown spotted) bananas (about 1 cup mashed)
2 eggs
¾ cup sugar
2/3 cup canola or vegetable oil
2/3 cup milk
1 teaspoon vanilla extract
1-2/3 cups flour
2 teaspoons ground cinnamon
1 ½ teaspoons baking powder
½ teaspoon salt
topping-
2 tablespoons sugar
½ teaspoon ground cinnamon

1. Preheat the oven to 350 degrees. Coat a 9x5-inch loaf pan with non-stick cooking spray. In a large mixing bowl, mash the bananas. Whisk in the eggs. Add the sugar, oil, milk and vanilla and whisk until blended.

2. Sift the flour, cinnamon, baking powder and salt over the bowl and gently whisk until the flour disappears (the batter will be lumpy).

3. Pour and spread the batter into the pan. Mix together the sugar and cinnamon and sprinkle over the batter. Bake for 35-40 minutes or until a toothpick comes out dry when inserted into the center.

Banana Bread with Chocolate Chips

Chocolate brings out the best in bananas.

3 very ripe (brown spotted) bananas (about 1 cup mashed)
2 eggs
½ cup sugar
½ cup canola or vegetable oil
2/3 cup milk
1 teaspoon vanilla extract
1-2/3 cups flour
1 teaspoon ground cinnamon
2 teaspoons baking powder
½ teaspoon salt
¾ cup semi-sweet chocolate chips
topping-
2 teaspoons sugar
2 teaspoons brown sugar

1. Preheat the oven to 350 degrees. Coat a 9x5-inch loaf pan with non-stick cooking spray. In a large mixing bowl, mash the bananas. Whisk in the eggs. Add the sugar, oil, milk and vanilla and whisk until blended.

2. Sift the flour, cinnamon, baking powder and salt over the bowl and gently whisk until the flour disappears (the batter will be lumpy). Gently fold in the chocolate chips.

3. Pour the batter into the pan. Mix the sugar and brown sugar together and sprinkle over the top. Bake for 40-45 minutes or until the bread turns brown and a toothpick comes out dry when inserted into the center.

Lemon-Glazed Blueberry Bread

A tart summer treat.

2 eggs
¾ cup sugar
2/3 cup canola or vegetable oil
2/3 cup milk
2 teaspoons lemon extract
1 teaspoon vanilla extract
1-2/3 cups flour
1 ½ teaspoons baking powder
½ teaspoon salt
1 cup blueberries tossed with 2 teaspoons flour
glaze-
1 cup confectioners' sugar
2 tablespoons warm milk
¼ teaspoon lemon extract

1. Preheat the oven to 350 degrees. Coat a 9x5-inch loaf pan with non-stick cooking spray. In a large mixing bowl, whisk the eggs. Add the sugar, oil, milk and extracts and whisk until blended.

2. Sift the flour, baking powder and salt over the bowl and gently whisk until the flour disappears (the batter will be lumpy). Gently fold in the flour-coated blueberries.

3. Pour the batter into the pan and bake for 35-45 minutes or until a toothpick comes out dry when inserted into the center. To make the glaze, whisk the confectioners' sugar, warm milk and lemon extract until smooth (add a more milk if too stiff, more sugar if too runny). Pour over the cooled bread.

Cinnamon Zucchini Bread

A wonderful anytime treat.

2 eggs
¾ cup sugar
2/3 cup canola or vegetable oil
1 teaspoon vanilla extract
1-2/3 cups flour
2 teaspoons ground cinnamon
1 ½ teaspoons baking powder
½ teaspoon salt
1 ½ cups grated zucchini
topping-
2 tablespoons sugar
½ teaspoon ground cinnamon

1. Preheat the oven to 350 degrees. Coat a 9x5-inch loaf pan with non-stick cooking spray. In a large mixing bowl, whisk the eggs. Add the sugar, oil and vanilla and whisk until blended.

2. Sift the flour, cinnamon, baking powder and salt over the bowl and gently whisk until the flour disappears (the batter will be lumpy). Gently fold in the grated zucchini.

3. Pour and spread the batter into the pan. Blend the sugar and cinnamon together and sprinkle over the top. Bake for 35-45 minutes or until the top turns brown and a toothpick comes out dry when inserted into the center.

Vanilla-Buttered Cornbread

Just Like Traditional Cornbread, Only Better!

2 eggs
¼ cup sugar
1 cup cornmeal
½ cup canola or vegetable oil
1 ¼ cups warm milk
1 teaspoon vanilla extract
1 cup flour
2 teaspoons baking powder
½ teaspoon salt
topping-
½ teaspoon vanilla extract
¼ cup (half a stick) melted butter
1 tablespoon sugar

1. Preheat the oven to 350 degrees. Coat an 8-inch square or a 9-inch round baking pan with non-stick cooking spray. In a large mixing bowl, whisk the eggs. Add the sugar, cornmeal, oil, warm milk and vanilla and whisk until blended.

2. Sift the flour, baking powder and salt over the bowl and gently whisk until the flour disappears.

3. Pour and spread the batter into pan. For the topping, stir the vanilla into the melted butter and pour over the batter. Sprinkle the top with sugar. Bake for 25-30 minutes or until the cornbread turns brown around the edges and a toothpick comes out dry when inserted into the center.

Breakfast Banana Bread

Wholesome and delicious.

3 very ripe (brown spotted) bananas (about 1 cup mashed)
2 eggs
1 cup sugar
2/3 cup canola or vegetable oil
1 cup plain yogurt
1 teaspoon vanilla extract
1 cup oats
1 ½ cups flour
2 teaspoons ground cinnamon
1 ½ teaspoons baking powder
½ teaspoon salt

1.   Preheat the oven to 350 degrees. Coat a 9x5-inch loaf pan with non-stick cooking spray. In a large mixing bowl, mash the bananas. Whisk in the eggs. Add the sugar, oil, yogurt and vanilla and whisk until blended. Stir in the oats.

2.   Sift the flour, cinnamon, baking powder and salt over the bowl and gently whisk until the flour disappears (the batter will be lumpy).

3.   Pour the batter into the pan and bake for 40-45 minutes or until the bread turns brown and a toothpick comes out dry when inserted into the center.

Granola Breakfast Muffins

Perfect in the morning with a spread of butter and jam.

2 eggs
2/3 cup sugar
½ cup canola or vegetable oil
1 cup plain yogurt
1 teaspoon vanilla extract
1 ½ cups granola cereal
1 ¾ cups flour
1 teaspoon cinnamon
2 teaspoons baking powder
½ teaspoon salt

1. Preheat the oven to 375 degrees. Coat a 12-cup muffin pan with non-stick cooking spray. In a large mixing bowl, whisk the eggs. Add the sugar, oil, yogurt and vanilla and whisk until blended. Stir in the granola.

2. Sift the flour, cinnamon, baking powder and salt over the bowl and gently whisk until the flour disappears (the batter will be lumpy).

3. Use a quarter-cup measure to spoon the batter into the muffin cups. Bake for 18-20 minutes or until a toothpick comes out dry when inserted into the center.

Breakfast Bars

These make a tasty and wholesome breakfast or anytime snack.

2 eggs
1 cup brown sugar
½ cup canola or vegetable oil
1 cup plain yogurt
1 cup flour
2 teaspoons ground cinnamon
¼ teaspoon baking soda
½ teaspoon salt
2 cups oats
1 cup toasted oat cereal (like Cheerios)
½ cup granola
½ cup chopped walnuts or almonds

1. Preheat the oven to 350 degrees. Coat a 9x13-inch baking pan with non-stick cooking spray. In a large mixing bowl, whisk the eggs. Add the brown sugar, oil and yogurt and whisk until blended.

2. Sift the flour, cinnamon, baking soda and salt over the bowl and whisk until smooth. Stir in the oats, cereal, granola and almonds.

3. Pour and spread the mixture into the pan and bake for 18-20 minutes or until the edges are brown and the center begins to turn brown.

Simple Scones

Spruce these up with chocolate, nuts or fruit.

2 cups flour
½ cup sugar
2 teaspoons baking powder
½ teaspoon salt (omit if using salted butter)
10 tablespoons (1 stick plus 2 tablespoons) butter, melted
1 egg, beaten
1/3 cup milk
1 teaspoon vanilla extract
¾ cup chocolate chips, chopped nuts, dried fruit or berries
additional sugar for topping

1. Preheat the oven to 375 degrees. Coat a baking sheet with non-stick cooking spray or line with parchment paper. In a large mixing bowl, whisk the flour, sugar, baking powder and salt.

2. Add the melted butter, beaten egg, milk and vanilla and gently stir until the dry ingredients are moistened (the batter will be lumpy). Gently fold in the chocolate, nuts or fruit, if using.

3. Pour the batter onto the baking sheet and with floured hands, shape the dough into an 8-inch circle. With a large knife or pizza cutter dipped in flour, cut the circle into 8 wedges (like a pizza) and separate the slices about a quarter inch. Sprinkle the circle of scones with 1 tablespoon of sugar. Bake for 16-18 minutes or until they turn light brown.

Cranberry Biscuit Scones

Perfect for a fall feast.

2 cups flour
½ cup sugar
2 teaspoons baking powder
½ teaspoon salt (omit if using salted butter)
½ cup (1 stick) butter, melted
1 egg, beaten
1 cup whole berry cranberry sauce
1 tablespoon additional sugar for tops

1. Preheat the oven to 375 degrees. Coat a baking sheet with non-stick cooking spray or line with parchment paper. In a large mixing bowl, whisk the flour, sugar, baking powder and salt.

2. Add the melted butter, beaten egg and cranberry sauce to the bowl and gently whisk until the dry ingredients are moistened (the batter will be lumpy).

3. Pour the batter onto the baking sheet and with floured hands, shape the dough into an 8-inch circle. With a large knife or pizza cutter dipped in flour, cut the circle into 8 wedges (like a pizza) and separate the slices about a quarter inch. Sprinkle the circle of scones with 1 tablespoon of sugar. Bake for 16-18 minutes or until they turn light brown.

Quick-Fix French Toast Casserole

Whip this up now and bake it tomorrow morning for an easy and delicious breakfast.

1 large loaf of day old French bread
7 eggs
3 cups milk
2 teaspoons vanilla extract
¼ cup sugar
½ teaspoon salt
topping-
½ cup (1 stick) butter
¼ cup sugar
1 teaspoon ground cinnamon

1. Coat a 9x13-inch baking dish with non-stick cooking spray. Cut the bread into three-quarter inch slices and layer the slices in slanted rows, covering the bottom of the pan.

2. In a large mixing bowl, whisk the eggs. Add the milk, vanilla, sugar and salt and whisk until blended. Pour over the bread. Cut the stick of butter into about 12 pats and spread them out on top of the bread. Mix the sugar and cinnamon together and sprinkle over the top. Cover the dish and refrigerate overnight.

3. When you are ready to bake, preheat the oven to 350 degrees. Set the casserole into the oven and bake for 45-55 minutes or until the casserole is golden brown and bubbling. Serve with soft butter and maple syrup.

Classic French Toast

No better way to start the day.

4 eggs
1 cup warm milk
1 teaspoon vanilla extract
2 tablespoons sugar
6-8 slices (depending on size) dry bread

1. In a large mixing bowl, whisk the eggs. Add the warm milk, vanilla and sugar and whisk until blended. Soak each slice of bread in the batter, one at a time, until the bread becomes saturated.

2. Melt some butter in a large non-stick skillet over medium-high heat. Place the slices of soaked bread onto the skillet and fry until the bottom of the bread turns golden brown. Flip over and fry the other side until brown. (Reduce the heat if the bread is cooking too quickly.)

3. Serve immediately or place into a warm oven until ready to serve. Enjoy with soft butter and maple syrup. (These can be wrapped and stored in the refrigerator. Then pop them into the toaster anytime to make them warm and crisp.)

Classic American Pancakes

Just like the ones from the local pancake house.

2 eggs
1 ½ cups warm milk
¼ cup sugar
1 teaspoon vanilla extract
2 cups flour
2 teaspoons baking powder
½ teaspoon salt
6 tablespoons melted butter

1. In a large mixing bowl, whisk the eggs. Add the warm milk, sugar and vanilla and whisk until blended. Sift the flour, baking powder and salt over the bowl and gently whisk until the flour disappears (the batter will be lumpy). Fold in the melted butter.

2. Melt some butter on a griddle or skillet over a medium heat. Pour quarter-cupfuls of the batter onto the pan and cook until small bubbles form and begin to pop on the tops of the pancakes. Flip and cook until golden brown on the other side. (Reduce the heat if pancakes are browning too quickly.)

3. Serve with soft butter and maple syrup. (These can be wrapped and stored in the refrigerator. Then pop them into the toaster anytime to make them warm and crisp.)

Blueberry-Buttermilk Sunshine Pancakes

Orange juice and tart blueberries in these pancakes will brighten your day.

2 eggs
¼ cup sugar
½ cup orange juice
¼ cup canola or vegetable oil
1 cup buttermilk
1 teaspoon vanilla extract
2 cups flour
2 teaspoons baking powder
½ teaspoon salt
1-2 cups blueberries (depending on how many you like to have in your pancakes)

1. In a large mixing bowl, whisk the eggs. Add the sugar, juice, oil, buttermilk and vanilla and whisk until blended. Sift the flour, baking powder and salt over the bowl and gently whisk until the flour disappears (the batter will be lumpy).

2. Melt some butter on a griddle or skillet over a medium heat. Pour quarter-cupfuls of the batter onto the pan, sprinkle the tops with some blueberries (pressing them down gently into the batter) and cook until the batter forms small bubbles that begin to pop. Flip and cook until golden brown on the other side. (Reduce the heat if pancakes are browning too quickly.)

3. Serve with soft butter and maple syrup. (These can be wrapped and stored in the refrigerator. Then pop them into the toaster anytime to make them warm and crisp.)

Classic Buttermilk Waffles

These luxurious waffles can be whipped up in no time.

3 eggs
¼ cup sugar
¼ cup canola or vegetable oil
1-2/3 cups buttermilk
1 teaspoon vanilla extract
2 cups flour
2 teaspoons baking powder
½ teaspoon salt

1. In a large mixing bowl, whisk the eggs. Add the sugar, oil, buttermilk and vanilla and whisk until blended.

2. Sift the flour, baking powder and salt over the bowl and gently whisk until the flour disappears (the batter will be lumpy).

3. Spoon the batter onto a pre-heated waffle iron coated with non-stick cooking spray. Cook until the waffles are light brown and crisp. Serve with soft butter and maple syrup. (These can be wrapped and stored in the refrigerator. Then pop them into the toaster anytime to make them warm and crisp.)

Very Chocolate Waffles

These are extra-special topped with chocolate sauce and whipped cream.

2 eggs
¼ cup canola or vegetable oil
1/3 cup sugar
1 ½ cups buttermilk
1 teaspoon vanilla extract
1 ½ cups flour
½ cup unsweetened cocoa powder
1 ½ teaspoons baking powder
½ teaspoon salt
1 cup semi-sweet chocolate chips

1. In a large mixing bowl, whisk the eggs. Add the oil, sugar, buttermilk and vanilla and whisk until blended.

2. Sift the flour, cocoa powder, baking powder and salt over the bowl and gently whisk until the dry ingredients disappear. (The batter will be lumpy. Pour in a little more buttermilk if the batter is too stiff.) Gently fold in the chocolate chips.

3. Preheat a waffle iron and coat with non-stick cooking spray. Spoon the batter onto the waffle iron and cook until waffles are firm and cooked through.

Coffee Cake Crescents

Make the filling ahead of time and you'll always be minutes away from fresh baked pastry.

1/3 cup flour
1/3 cup brown sugar
1 teaspoon ground cinnamon
½ teaspoon vanilla extract
4 tablespoons melted butter
1/3 cup chopped pecans
1-8 ounce package refrigerated crescent rolls

1. Preheat the oven to 375 degrees. In a large mixing bowl, whisk together the flour, brown sugar and cinnamon. Mix the vanilla into the melted butter and stir into the mixture. Stir in the pecans.

2. Open and unroll the dough. Spoon and spread 2 tablespoons of the mixture over each triangle of dough. Roll up each piece starting with the long edge (bottom) of the triangle.

3. Place each crescent onto a baking sheet with the tip of the triangle set downward on the sheet. Bend the outer edges of each one to make a crescent shape. Bake for 10 minutes or until the crescents turn light golden brown.

Fast and Friendly Fruit Desserts

Vanilla-Buttered Blueberry Cobbler

A ravishing cobbler recipe.

3 heaping cups blueberries
3 tablespoons butter, melted
1 teaspoon vanilla extract
2 teaspoons cornstarch
1/3 cup sugar (1-2 teaspoons more if berries are not very sweet)
top-
1 cup flour
½ cup sugar
1 teaspoon baking powder
¼ teaspoon salt (omit if using salted butter)
5 tablespoons butter, melted
1 teaspoon vanilla extract
½ cup warm milk

1. Preheat the oven to 375 degrees. Coat an 8-inch square or 2-quart baking dish with non-stick cooking spray. Place the blueberries in a large bowl. Stir the vanilla extract into the melted butter, pour over the berries and gently toss until berries are coated. With a fork or small whisk, blend the cornstarch into the sugar and stir into the berries. Pour and spread the berries into the pan and set aside.

2. In a large mixing bowl, whisk the flour, sugar, baking powder and salt. Add the melted butter and vanilla and stir until the mixture is crumbly. Gently fold in the milk (the batter should be lumpy).

3. Place 9-large spoonfuls of the batter on top of the berries, creating a patchwork design. (Spread the dough so it is not more than three-quarters of an inch thick. Some of the blueberries should be exposed.) Bake for 25-30 minutes or until the biscuit topping is light brown and the blueberries are bubbling. Serve warm with vanilla ice cream or whipped cream.

Classic Cherry Cobbler

Sweet, soft cherries coddled in a cake topping.

¼ cup sugar
1 tablespoon cornstarch
2 ½ cups pitted cherries
1 teaspoon vanilla extract
1 ¼ cups flour
½ cup sugar
1 teaspoon baking powder
¼ teaspoon salt (omit if using salted butter)
6 tablespoons butter, melted
½ cup milk

1. Preheat the oven to 375 degrees. Coat an 8-inch square or 2-quart baking pan with non-stick cooking spray. In a medium-sized saucepan, whisk the sugar and cornstarch. Stir in the pitted cherries and bring the mixture to a boil over medium-high heat, stirring frequently. Remove from heat and stir in the vanilla.

2. In a large mixing bowl, whisk the flour, sugar, baking powder and salt. Add the melted butter and milk and gently stir until well combined and crumbly.

3. Pour the cherries into the pan. Place 9-large spoonfuls of the batter on top of the berries, creating a patchwork design. (Spread the dough so it is not more than three-quarters of an inch thick. Some of the cherries should be exposed.) Bake for 25-30 minutes or until the topping has turned light brown. Serve warm with vanilla ice cream or whipped cream.

Chewy Chocolate Cherry Crisp

Delightfully decadent.

½ cup sugar
2 tablespoons flour
2 cups pitted cherries
topping-
¾ cup flour
½ cup sugar
¼ teaspoon salt (omit if using salted butter)
½ cup oats
6 tablespoons butter, melted
1 cup semi-sweet chocolate chips

1. Preheat the oven to 375 degrees. Coat an 8-inch square or 2-quart baking pan with non-stick cooking spray. In a large mixing bowl, whisk the sugar and flour. Add the cherries and toss until evenly coated. Pour and spread evenly into the pan.

2. To make the topping, whisk together the flour, sugar and salt. Stir in the oats. Pour in the melted butter and stir until well combined and crumbly. Sprinkle over the cherry mixture. Top with the chocolate chips.

3. Bake for 25-30 minutes or until light brown and bubbly. Serve warm with vanilla ice cream or whipped cream.

Apple Crisp

Baked apples with a kiss of orange and vanilla.

4 cups sliced apples (about 6 apples, peeled, cored and cut into half-inch slices)
1 teaspoon vanilla extract
2 tablespoons orange juice
1 ¼ cups flour
1/3 cup sugar
1/3 cup brown sugar
1 teaspoon ground cinnamon
¼ teaspoon salt (omit if using salted butter)
6 tablespoons butter, melted

1. Preheat the oven to 350 degrees. Coat an 8-inch square baking pan or 2-quart baking dish with non-stick cooking spray. Place apple slices in a large bowl. Stir the vanilla into the orange juice, pour over the apples and toss until coated.

2. Whisk together the flour, sugar, brown sugar, cinnamon and salt. Pour in the melted butter and gently stir until well combined and crumbly. Pour and spread over the apples.

3. Bake for 30-35 minutes or until the top turns brown and the apples are bubbling. Serve warm with whipped cream or vanilla ice cream.

Peach Crisp

A simple summertime treat.

3 cups sliced peaches
1 teaspoon ground cinnamon
2 tablespoons sugar
topping-
1 ¼ cups flour
½ cup sugar
½ cup brown sugar
¼ teaspoon salt (omit if using salted butter)
1 teaspoon vanilla extract
6 tablespoons butter, melted

1. Preheat the oven to 375 degrees. Coat an 8-inch square or 2-quart baking dish with non-stick cooking spray. Pour and spread the peach slices into the pan. Blend the cinnamon and sugar together and sprinkle <u>1 tablespoon</u> of the mixture over the peaches.

2. In a large mixing bowl, whisk the flour, sugar, brown sugar and salt. Stir the vanilla into the melted butter and pour into the flour mixture. Gently stir until well combined and crumbly.

3. Pour and spread the topping evenly over the peaches. Sprinkle the top with the remaining tablespoon of cinnamon-sugar. Bake for 30-35 minutes or until topping turns light brown.

Rustic Cherry Crumble

Made with oats, cinnamon and cherry pie filling.

1 cup flour
¾ cup brown sugar
½ teaspoon ground cinnamon
½ teaspoon salt (omit if using salted butter)
¾ cup oats
½ teaspoon vanilla extract
¾ cup (1 ½ sticks) butter, melted
1-21 ounce can cherry pie filling

1. Preheat the oven to 375 degrees. Coat an 8-inch square or 2-quart baking dish with non-stick cooking spray. In a large mixing bowl, whisk the flour, brown sugar, cinnamon and salt. Stir in the oats.

2. Stir the vanilla to the melted butter. Add to the bowl and stir until the mixture is well combined and crumbly. Pour and spread half of the mixture into the bottom of the pan.

3. Pour and spread the cherry filling over the bottom layer. Sprinkle the top with the rest of the crumble mixture. Bake for 35-40 minutes or until the top turns light brown and the cherry filling is bubbling. Serve with vanilla ice cream or whipped cream.

Easy Fruit Crumble

Toss bits of apples, peaches, blueberries, cherries-any fruit you wish-into this recipe.

4 cups fruit, cut into bite-sized pieces
1 cup flour
½ cup sugar
½ cup brown sugar
1 teaspoon ground cinnamon
¼ teaspoon salt (omit if using salted butter)
6 tablespoons butter, melted
1 teaspoon vanilla extract

1. Preheat the oven to 375 degrees. Coat an 8-inch square baking pan or a 2-quart baking dish with non-stick cooking spray. Pour and spread the fruit into the pan.

2. In a large mixing bowl, whisk the flour, sugar, brown sugar, cinnamon and salt. Stir the vanilla to the melted butter and pour into the bowl. Gently stir until the mixture is well combined and crumbly.

3. Sprinkle the mixture over the fruit and press down gently. Bake for 30-35 minutes or until the top is light brown and bubbly. Serve warm with fresh whipped cream or vanilla ice cream.

Quick Peach Pastry

So quick, so easy and so tasty.

1-8 ounce can refrigerated crescent rolls (makes 8 pastries)
3 tablespoons sugar
½ teaspoon ground cinnamon
1-15 ounce can of peach halves, drained and cut into 2 pieces

1. Preheat the oven to 375 degrees. Open the can and unroll the dough. In a small bowl, blend the sugar and cinnamon together. Sprinkle each triangle of dough with one-half teaspoon of the cinnamon-sugar.

2. Place a peach quarter at the base (large end) of each triangle. Roll up the dough starting with the base of the triangle and set it on a nonstick baking sheet with the tip of the triangle pressed down on the sheet.

3. Sprinkle the top of each crescent with one-half teaspoon of the cinnamon sugar and bake for 10-12 minutes or until the tops turn light brown.

Fresh Berry Cake

Soft cake bursting with fresh berry flavor.

2 eggs
¾ cup sugar
1 teaspoon vanilla extract
6 tablespoons butter, melted
1 tablespoon fresh lemon juice
1 ¼ cups sifted flour
1 teaspoon baking powder
¼ teaspoon salt (omit if using salted butter)
2 cups fresh berries (strawberries, blueberries raspberries, blackberries …)
confectioners' sugar

1. Preheat the oven to 350 degrees. Coat an 8-inch square or 9-inch round baking pan with non-stick cooking spray. In a large mixing bowl, whisk the eggs. Add the sugar, vanilla and melted butter and whisk until smooth. Stir in the lemon juice.

2. Sift the flour, baking powder and salt over the bowl and gently whisk until the flour disappears (the batter will be lumpy).

3. Pour the batter into the pan and sprinkle the berries evenly over the top. Bake for 25-30 minutes or until the cake turns light brown and a toothpick comes out dry when inserted into center. Sift confectioners' sugar over the top when cake has cooled. Serve with whipped cream or vanilla ice cream.

Apple Crumble Pie

Simple ingredients let apples shine in this easy pie recipe.

5 cups apple slices (about one-half inch thick)
2 teaspoon vanilla extract
1 teaspoon ground cinnamon
1/3 cup sugar
1—9 inch, deep dish, ready-made pie crust
topping-
1 cup flour
½ cup sugar
1 teaspoon ground cinnamon
¼ teaspoon salt (omit if using salted butter)
6 tablespoons butter, melted

1. Preheat the oven to 350 degrees. In a large mixing bowl, toss the apples with the vanilla. Stir the cinnamon into the sugar, pour over the apples and toss until evenly coated. Pour and spread the apples into the pie crust.

2. To make the topping, whisk together the flour, sugar, cinnamon and salt. Add the melted butter and stir until well combined and crumbly. Sprinkle evenly over the apples and press down gently.

3. Place the pie on a foil-lined baking sheet (in case the pie juices bubble over). Bake for 40-50 minutes or until the pie is light brown and bubbly. Serve warm with vanilla ice cream or whipped cream.

Cinnamon-Maple Apple Dessert

Cinnamon and maple make apples irresistible.

4 cups sliced apples (cut one-half inch thick)
1 teaspoon vanilla extract
½ cup maple syrup
1 teaspoon ground cinnamon
1 egg
½ cup sugar
¼ cup milk
6 tablespoons butter, melted
1 cup flour
½ teaspoon baking powder
¼ teaspoon salt (omit if using salted butter)

1. Preheat the oven to 375 degrees. Coat an 8-inch square baking pan or 2-quart baking dish with non-stick cooking spray. Pour and spread the apples into the pan. Stir the vanilla extract into the maple syrup and pour over the apples. Sprinkle the cinnamon over the apples.

2. In a large mixing bowl, whisk the egg. Add the sugar, milk and melted butter and whisk until blended. Sift the flour, baking powder and salt over the bowl and gently whisk until the flour disappears (the batter will be lumpy).

3. Pour and spread the batter over the apples. (The apples will not be completely covered.) Bake for 25-30 minutes or until the top is light brown and bubbling. Serve warm with whipped cream or vanilla ice cream.

Classic Strawberry Shortcakes

Fresh-baked cake and whipped cream bring out the best in strawberries.

4 cups strawberries, cut into bite size pieces
4 tablespoons sugar
cakes-
1 egg
½ cup sugar
½ cup milk
1 teaspoon vanilla extract
½ cup (1 stick) butter, melted
1 ½ cups flour
1 teaspoon baking powder
½ teaspoon salt (omit if using salted butter)
2 cups (1-8oz. tub) whipped cream topping

1. Preheat the oven to 350 degrees. Toss the strawberries with the 4 table-spoons of sugar and set aside. In a large mixing bowl, whisk the egg. Add the sugar, milk, vanilla and melted butter and whisk until blended.

2. Sift the flour, baking powder and salt over the bowl and stir until the batter forms a lumpy dough. Divide the dough into 8 portions and set 2-inches apart onto a non-stick cookie sheet or cookie sheet lined with parchment paper. Flatten the tops just a bit and sprinkle each with half a teaspoon of sugar. Bake for 12-15 minutes or until they turn light brown.

3. When the shortcakes have cooled off, cut horizontally (like a hamburger bun), fill with about a half cup of strawberries, and top with a large dollop of whipped cream.

Peaches & Cream Muffi-Shortcakes

These cute little cakes are made in a muffin tin.

1 egg
½ cup sugar
1 teaspoon vanilla extract
2/3 cup milk
½ cup (1 stick) butter, melted
1 ½ cups flour
1 teaspoon baking powder
¼ teaspoon salt (omit if using salted butter)
1 large can sliced peaches (save the juice from the can)
2 cups (1—8oz. tub) whipped cream topping

1. Preheat the oven to 375 degrees. Coat a 12-cup muffin pan with non-stick cooking spray. In a large mixing bowl, whisk the egg. Add the sugar, vanilla, milk and melted butter and whisk until blended. Sift the flour, baking powder and salt over the bowl and gently whisk until the flour disappears (the batter will be lumpy).

2. Spoon the batter into the muffin cups. Bake for 15-18 minutes or until the tops begin to turn brown and a toothpick comes out dry when inserted into the center.

3. Cut off the top third of each muffin. Set several peach slices over the bottom half and drizzle a bit of peach juice from the can over the peaches. Set the muffin top back on and garnish with a large dollop of whipped cream.

Peach Brown Betty

An old-fashioned way to enjoy sunny peaches.

2 cups coarse bread crumbs
2/3 cup brown sugar
1 teaspoon cinnamon
¼ teaspoon salt (omit if using salted butter)
½ cup (1 stick) butter, melted
1 teaspoon vanilla extract
3 cups sliced peaches

1. Preheat the oven to 350 degrees. Coat an 8-inch square or 2-quart baking pan with non-stick cooking spray. Whisk together the breadcrumbs, brown sugar, cinnamon and salt.

2. Blend the vanilla into the melted butter, pour into the bowl, and gently stir until the mixture is well combined and crumbly.

3. Spread half of the mixture evenly on the bottom of the pan. Place the peaches over the crumb mixture and sprinkle the remaining crumb mixture over the top. Bake for 35-40 minutes or until the top is brown and bubbling. Serve warm with vanilla ice cream or whipped cream.

Blueberries n' Dumplings

This warm, delightful dessert is cooked in a saucepan.

¾ cup sugar
2 tablespoons cornstarch
½ cup water
4 cups blueberries
dumplings-
1 cup flour
3 tablespoons sugar
1 teaspoon baking powder
¼ teaspoon salt (omit if using salted butter)
5 tablespoons butter, melted
¼ cup milk
1 teaspoon vanilla extract

1. Whisk the sugar and cornstarch together in a 10-inch sauté pan. Add the water and whisk until well blended. Add the berries and stir over medium heat until the mixture thickens and comes to a gentle boil. Remove from the heat and set aside.

2. In a medium bowl, whisk together the flour, sugar, baking powder and salt. Add the melted butter, milk and vanilla and gently stir until a lumpy batter forms.

3. Bring the berry mixture to a steaming simmer over low heat and drop 6 rounded portions of the batter on top of the fruit. Cover the pan and continue cooking over medium-low heat for 10-15 minutes or until a toothpick comes out dry when inserted into the center of a dumpling. Serve warm with whipped cream or ice cream.

Apple Pandowdy

Cinnamon-sugared apples baked underneath a soft, simple cake.

1 tablespoon sugar
1 tablespoon brown sugar
½ teaspoon ground cinnamon
3 cups apple slices (cut into one-half inch slices)
top-
1 egg
1/3 cup sugar
1 teaspoon vanilla extract
4 tablespoons (half a stick) butter, melted
1/3 cup milk
1 cup flour
1 teaspoon baking powder
¼ teaspoon salt (omit if using salted butter)
1 tablespoon (additional) sugar

1. Preheat the oven to 350 degrees. Coat an 8-inch square baking pan or a 2-quart baking dish with non-stick cooking spray. In a large mixing bowl, whisk together the sugar, brown sugar and cinnamon. Add the sliced apples and toss until well coated. Pour into the bottom of the pan.

2. In a medium-sized mixing bowl, whisk the egg. Add the sugar, vanilla, melted butter and milk and whisk until blended. Sift the flour, baking powder and salt over the bowl and gently whisk until the flour disappears (the batter will be lumpy).

3. Pour and spread the batter over the apples. Sprinkle the top of the batter with 1 tablespoon of sugar. Bake for 30-35 minutes or until the topping turns brown. Serve warm with vanilla ice cream or whipped cream.

Vanilla-Sugared Peach Duff

Soft, moist cake bakes-up underneath vanilla-sugared peaches.

3 cups sliced peaches
2 teaspoons vanilla extract
1 cup flour
1 ¼ teaspoons baking powder
½ cup sugar
¼ teaspoon salt (omit if using salted butter)
2/3 cup milk
5 tablespoons butter, melted
1 tablespoon (additional) sugar

1. Preheat the oven to 350 degrees. Coat an 8-inch square baking pan or a 2-quart baking dish with non-stick cooking spray. In a large mixing bowl, toss the peaches with the vanilla. Set aside.

2. In a mixing bowl, whisk together the flour, baking powder, sugar and salt. Gently whisk in the milk until the flour disappears (the batter will be lumpy).

3. Pour and spread the batter into the pan. Pour the melted butter over the batter. Spread the peaches over the top and sprinkle with the additional tablespoon of sugar. Bake for 30-35 minutes or until the batter turns brown. Serve warm with vanilla ice cream or whipped cream.

Fresh Fruit Fool

A creamy, fruity treat.

3-4 cups fresh fruit (strawberries, blueberries, raspberries, cherries, mango, pineapple, banana ...)
½ cup sugar
2 cups (1-8 ounce tub) whipped cream topping, thawed

1. In a food processor or blender, blend the fruit until it turns into liquid. Add the sugar and blend again. (Add more sugar if you want it sweeter.)

2. Pour the whipped cream into a large bowl. Slowly fold the fruit into the cream until the fruit is evenly distributed but not completely blended within the cream. (You should see separate streaks of fruit and cream.)

3. Spoon the mixture into dessert glasses or a decorative serving dish. Garnish with shredded coconut, nuts, fruit or additional whipped cream, if desired. Makes 3-4 servings.

Really Fast Fruit Fool

Dessert doesn't get quicker than this.

1 can—about 20 ounces—fruit pie filling (strawberry, blueberry, cherry ...)
2 cups frozen whipped topping, thawed

1. Slowly fold the pie filling into the whipped topping until the fruit is evenly distributed but not completely blended within the cream. (You should see separate streaks of fruit and cream.)

2. Spoon the mixture into dessert glasses or a decorative serving dish. Garnish with shredded coconut, nuts, fresh fruit or additional whipped cream, if desired. Makes 3-4 servings.

Fresh Strawberry Trifle

If it's strawberry season, this is the dessert to make.

2–16 ounce packages fresh strawberries
2–3.5 ounce boxes vanilla pudding mix, plus ingredients to prepare
2–12 ounce store-bought pound cakes
½ cup sliced almond pieces
2–8 ounce tubs whipped topping, thawed

1. Wash the berries, remove the green tops, and cut into bite-sized pieces. (Set aside a big, pretty strawberry to garnish the top.) Prepare the pudding and set aside. Cut the cake into bite-sized cubes.

2. In the bottom of a deep serving bowl or glass trifle dish, spread half of the cake cubes. Pour and spread half of the pudding over the cake. Sprinkle with half of the berries, then sprinkle with half of the sliced almonds. Then pour and spread 1 tub of whipped cream over the top.

3. Repeat the 5 layers (cake-pudding-strawberries-almonds-cream). Garnish the top with a big strawberry. Cover and keep refrigerated until ready to serve.

Pineapple-Cherry Trifle

A scrumptious dessert that looks as good as it tastes.

2–3.5 ounce boxes vanilla pudding mix, plus ingredients to prepare
2–12 ounce store-bought pound cakes
½ cup chopped maraschino cherries, plus 1 whole cherry for garnish
2–20 ounce cans crushed pineapple, drained
½ cup sliced almond pieces
2–8 ounce tubs whipped topping, thawed

1. Prepare the pudding and set aside. Cut the cake into bite-sized cubes. Stir the chopped cherries into the drained pineapple.

2. In the bottom of a deep serving bowl or glass trifle dish, spread half of the cake cubes. Pour and spread half of the pudding over the cake. Sprinkle with half of the pineapple-cherry mixture. Sprinkle with half of the sliced almonds. Then pour and spread 1 tub (2 cups) of the whipped cream over the top.

3. Repeat the 5 layers one more time (cake-pudding-pineapple-almonds-cream). Garnish with the whole cherry. Cover and keep refrigerated until ready to serve.

One-Pan Blueberry-Peach Trifle

Boxed pudding and cake mixes lets you enjoy fresh summer fruit in a jiffy.

1–4.6 ounce package "Cook and Serve" vanilla pudding mix (plus ingredients to prepare)
3 tablespoons cream cheese, softened
2 cups sliced peaches
2 cups fresh blueberries
3 cups whipped cream (1 ½–8 ounce tubs frozen whipped topping, thawed)
1 box white cake mix, prepared and baked in a 9x13-inch pan

1. Cook the pudding according to the package directions, remove from heat and stir in the cream cheese. Set aside to cool.

2. Spread the peaches and blueberries over the top of the baked cake. Pour and spread the pudding mixture over the fruit. Cover with the whipped cream.

3. Garnish with extra blueberries and peaches, if desired. Cover and chill until ready to serve.

A List of Ingredient Substitutions

Butter—If you don't have any on hand, you might have some luck using a butter substitute, margarine or shortening but it will likely change the consistency of your recipe. Go ahead and give it a try. Just be sure not to substitute butter with liquid oils.

Salted and Unsalted Butter—Most baking recipes call for unsalted butter because of the inconsistent salt content in different brands. Plus, many find that unsalted just tastes fresher than salted. If you only have salted butter, then go ahead and use it. Just don't add salt to the recipe. When using unsalted butter, add the salt called for in the recipe.

Brown Sugar—Brown sugar is nothing more than white sugar mixed with molasses. For 1/3 cup of brown sugar, blend 1 teaspoon of molasses with one-third cup of white sugar. Or, blend 1 tablespoon of molasses with 1 cup of white sugar to make 1 cup of brown sugar.

Baking Powder—For 1 teaspoon of baking powder, combine ½ teaspoon baking soda with 1 teaspoon cream of tartar. Or, use baking soda instead and add 2 teaspoons of white distilled vinegar for every ½ teaspoon of baking soda added to the recipe.

Cream—For 1 cup of cream, melt 1 tablespoon of butter and stir it into 1 cup of whole milk.

Buttermilk—For 1 cup of buttermilk, stir 1 tablespoon of lemon juice or white distilled vinegar into lukewarm milk to measure 1 cup.

Sour Cream—substitute with plain yogurt, buttermilk or cream (see cream and buttermilk substitutions).

Eggs—Egg substitutes from a carton will work. Just follow the instructions on the side of the package for the equivalent of eggs called for in the recipe.

Sugar—Nothing can adequately replace this sweet stuff. Check again. Maybe there is some hiding in the back of the pantry or in the sugar bowl.

Flour—Sorry, no substitution here either. You'll have to make yourself presentable and run to the store. Of course you could always go ask a neighbor.

Don't be afraid to borrow from a neighbor. You can always bring them over a sampling of your recipe to thank them!

978-0-595-45187-0
0-595-45187-X